HMS CENTAUR
1943 – 1972

Neil McCart

HMS CENTAUR
1943 – 1972

Neil McCart

FOREWORD BY
REAR-ADMIRAL O. H. M. ST JOHN STEINER CB

HMS *Centaur* during the 1950s making a lot of black smoke.

(Fleet Air Arm Museum)

To all ex-*Centaurs* 1954-1965

Front Cover: A magnificent watercolour painting of HMS *Centaur* by artist Brian Conroy, Greatham, Hampshire.

Cover Design by Caroline McCart
© Neil McCart/FAN PUBLICATIONS 1997
ISBN: 0 9519538 9 3

Typesetting By: Highlight Type Bureau Ltd,
Clifton House, 2 Clifton Villas,
Bradford, West Yorkshire BD8 7BY

Printing By: The Amadeus Press Ltd,
517 Leeds Road, Huddersfield,
West Yorkshire HD2 1YJ

Published By FAN PUBLICATIONS
17 Wymans Lane, Cheltenham, GL51 9QA, England. Fax & Tel 01242 580290

Contents

Foreword

It gives me a lot of pleasure to write a short foreword for such a thorough and carefully researched book by Neil McCart - easily read and well illustrated.

It was a great privilege to command HMS *Centaur* for nearly two and a half years in what was to be her last commission.

She was a very happy ship and, as a result, a very efficient ship. I had a splendid ship's company and aircrew who cheerfully did all, and more, that was asked of them. We trusted one another and they never let me down.

I am sure that she was equally good with my illustrious predecessors. Actions speak louder than words.

My most sincere thanks to those who served with me and to Neil McCart's vivid and lasting tribute to a marvellous ship.

O. H. M. St John Steiner CB
Rear-Admiral

Chapter One

The Builder's Yard

On 12 July 1943 the Director of Naval Contracts placed an order number CP8/84862/43/V.64B with the Belfast shipbuilding company of Harland & Wolff, at their Queen's Island works, for the construction of one light fleet carrier. It was intended that the carrier would be one of a class of eight ships which would be much improved versions of the Colossus class, the construction of which was begun in June 1942. She was to be named *Centaur*, the other seven being *Albion*, *Elephant*, *Bulwark*, *Hermes*, *Arrogant*, *Monmouth* and *Polyphemus*. In the event the latter four ships never left the drawing board as their contracts were cancelled at the end of the Second World War, and the *Elephant* was renamed *Hermes*.

By July 1943 North Africa had been cleared of Axis forces and Allied troops had successfully broken out from their beachheads following the invasion of Sicily. However,

The *Centaur* on the stocks at Belfast. Her hangar is under construction and the forward lift well can be seen.
(Ulster Folk & Transport Museum)

it was on the steppes of Russia that the mighty German Army finally met its match, and on the day that the Admiralty placed the order for the *Centaur* Russian troops began their massive counter-offensive around the Kursk salient. Near the village of Prochorovka the largest tank battle in history was fought, with the Germans losing over 400 of their tanks.

It was in the Indian and Pacific Oceans that aircraft carriers had proved themselves to be the new capital ships. Operating in self-contained task forces and using tactics which had been perfected by the US Navy, the carriers covered vast distances of ocean and could remain at sea for weeks on end. With a mix of Torpedo Bomber Reconnaissance (TBR) and All Weather Fighter (FAW) aircraft, aircraft carriers were undoubtedly formidable warships, and with no end in sight to the war against Japan there was a distinct possibility that the *Centaur* would join the British Pacific Fleet for, following the surrender of the Italian Fleet in September 1943, the opportunity arose for a British naval force to steam east. The British Government had prevailed upon the United States to allow a British Pacific Fleet to fight alongside the US Fleet in the Pacific. The Royal Navy's light fleet carriers were the Admiralty's solution to overcoming Britain's limited shipbuilding resources. The idea and design for these smaller versions of the fleet aircraft carrier were devised during the Second World War, but only a few of them were completed in time to take part in the closing stages of that conflict. However, they proved to be an outstanding success in the post-war years and they served six of the world's navies.

The first keel plates for the *Centaur* were laid on 30 May 1944 and construction work continued until the war ended 16 months later, whereupon the building of merchant ships became the new priority. It was at this time that contracts for four of the Centaur-class vessels, *Hermes*, *Arrogant*, *Monmouth* and *Polyphemus*, were cancelled, and the *Elephant*, which was under construction at Vickers Armstrong's Barrow-in-Furness shipyard, was renamed *Hermes*. It would be late 1959 before this carrier was eventually commissioned and by then her design had been modified so many times that she was virtually unrecognizable as one of the Centaur class. For almost two years after the end of the war work continued very slowly on the *Centaur*, and the first that the public knew of the progress came on Wednesday 16 April 1947, when Mr W. J. Edwards, the Civil Lord of the Admiralty, announced that the light fleet carrier was to be launched the following

Workers at Harland & Wolff's shipyard rush forward as the *Centaur* slides down the slipway and enters the water for the first time.

(Ulster Folk & Transport Museum)

For two and a half years after her launch the *Centaur* was laid up at Harland & Wolff's shipyard. In this photograph she is on the left of the picture, alongside HMS *Bulwark* which has not been there quite so long. In the background HMS *Eagle* is under construction.

(Ulster Folk & Transport Museum)

week by Her Royal Highness The Duchess of Kent. However, the launch was performed only in order to clear a slipway for the building of a new Union Castle Line passenger ship, and there were no plans to complete the naval vessel in the immediate future. The launching ceremony took place at midday on Tuesday 22 April 1947 and the Duchess of Kent, who was on a four-day visit to Northern Ireland, arrived at the shipyard after having visited a hospital and a linen factory. Despite the short notice, large crowds turned out to witness the event and, as was the custom, all work at the shipyard ceased as the new ship took to the water. As the *Centaur* thundered down into the Victoria Channel, the assembled visitors and workers cheered her on her way, many of the workmen being perched high in the gantries overlooking the slipway. As the tugs took charge of the hull and prepared to tow her round to her lay-up berth in the Musgrave Channel, the VIPs and special guests were entertained to lunch by the chairman of Harland & Wolff, Sir Frederick Rebbeck, where he

proposed a toast to the Duchess and presented her with a box of Ulster linen as a memento of the occasion. In replying, the Duchess indicated the true reason for the launch of the *Centaur* when during her speech she declared, 'The restoration of our merchant fleet is of the greatest importance, and the more ships which can be built the better it will be for everyone.' By the time the Duchess left Harland & Wolff's shipyard later that afternoon the *Centaur* had been moored in her lay-up berth, where she would remain for the next two and a half years.

Throughout this time advancements in naval aviation were being made at a pace which left the post-war building programme behind, the two most important developments, both of which were British, being the mirror landing aid and the angled flight deck. The former was the invention of Lt-Cdr Nicholas Goodhart RN, who had come up with the idea as a result of the difficulties which the Deck Landing Control Officers (batsmen) had in communicating their hand signals to the pilots of jet

An interesting aerial view of the *Centaur* in Bangor Bay shortly after her completion and during her acceptance trials in September 1953. Originally she had an axial flight deck with the code letter L. *(Fleet Air Arm Museum)*

aircraft who had to react instantly when landing at speeds of over 100 knots. Nick Goodhart's mirror landing guide consisted of an arrangement of lights which were reflected in a concave, gyro-stabilized mirror situated at the side of the flight deck. By observing the position of the reflected lights, the approaching pilot could tell whether he was coming in to land at the correct height, thereby monitoring his own landing and applying any corrections instantly. The angled flight deck was the brainchild of Captain Dennis R. F. Cambell DSC RN (later Rear-Admiral and Flag Officer Flying Training), who had qualified as a Fleet Air Arm pilot in the 1920s. It was in 1951 that he suggested that aircraft landing approaches could be angled to a degree which would allow pilots who failed to catch an arrester wire to 'bolt' under reapplied throttle over the port bow. Used in conjunction with the gyro-stabilized mirror landing sight, this meant the jet pilot could maintain a steady approach speed, and a direction which would give him a clear escape route, avoiding the deck park. Both of these inventions were exploited by the US Navy who first tried out and proved the value of the angled flight deck in the USS *Antietam* during 1953, using a 10°angled deck. The Royal Navy would have various flight decks angled between $5\frac{1}{2}°$ and $8\frac{1}{2}°$, but neither of these new developments would be incorporated into the *Centaur* before she left the builder's yard at Belfast.

On 22 June 1948 the *Centaur* was joined at her lay-up berth by the newly launched HMS *Bulwark*, whilst work was well advanced on the larger fleet aircraft carrier, HMS *Eagle*. With the *Albion* laid up on the River Tyne and the *Hermes* still on the stocks at Barrow-in-Furness, the four Centaur-class aircraft carriers seemed to face a very uncertain future. On 7 October 1949 the *Centaur* was moved into dry dock where her underwater hull was scraped and painted, an operation which lasted a week and cost the Admiralty an extra £3,457.18s.0d (£3,457.90) on the contract price. The *Centaur* returned to her berth alongside the *Bulwark* and just over 12 months later, in early 1951, the Admiralty ordered that her construction should be restarted and completed.

The *Centaur*, like her sister ships *Albion* and *Bulwark*, was a vessel of 28,118 tons, with an overall length of 737 feet and a beam of 128 feet. She was a twin-screw ship, powered by two sets of Parsons geared turbines which developed 80,000 SHP and gave her a speed of 28 knots, the steam for the turbines being supplied by four Admiralty three-drum superheat boilers. The *Centaur* would be home to 80 officers and 950 ratings, with an additional 50

The *Centaur* was the only ship of the class to be finished with an axial flight deck and she was very similar in appearance to the Colossus class of aircraft carriers. *(Fleet Air Arm Museum)*

A fine aerial view of the *Centaur* in Bangor Bay during her acceptance trials in 1953. *(Fleet Air Arm Museum)*

officers and 250 ratings of the embarked air squadrons, and the accommodation for the ship's company on board the *Centaur* was a great improvement upon that found in the Colossus class. All meals would be served in the main dining halls which left the mess decks solely for sleeping and recreation, and instead of the traditional hammocks, numbered 'standee' bunks, canvas and metal framed, were installed. These were made up as normal beds with hammock canvas and nettles laid under the mattresses, and when not in use the bunks were laced up with the bedding freshly made and secured by means of a link which was provided on the holding chain. Almost all messes down to and including those on 4 Deck had scuttles and were also fitted with thermotank ventilation systems with the familiar punkah louvres. Messes which were below 4 Deck did not have scuttles, but they were ventilated to the same standard as those on the decks above. For recreation whilst at sea a cinema could be rigged in the after lift well on most evenings and tombola was usually played on three nights a week in the main dining hall, where there was also a well-stocked fiction library. As an additional amenity there was a canteen and soda fountain, situated in 4G section and run by the NAAFI. It was estimated that 250 miles of electrical cable and 250,000 electrical connections were fitted in the ship, and there were more than 700 electric motors ranging from 100 horsepower motors for the two main lifts, to small motors for driving potato peelers and ice cream making machines.

By the end of March 1953 the *Centaur* was ready to undergo her contractor's sea trials in the Irish Sea, during which she was manned by Harland & Wolff's riggers and engineers with Captain McLaren, Harland & Wolff's trials master and a Clyde pilot, assisted by Captain Trace, a Belfast pilot. The trials lasted for a week and they were considered to be a complete success, with all the main and auxiliary machinery having been put through its paces. On 13 August 1953 Captain H. P. Sears RN was appointed as the *Centaur's* first commanding officer and in the following month the great majority of the ship's company joined the vessel, having travelled from Chatham Barracks. Captain Sears, who was the son of a Canon of Gloucester, had joined the Navy in 1921 and six years later he had qualified as a pilot. In 1950-51 he was the commanding officer of RNAS Ford, near Arundel, and after that he became Captain (Air) on the staff of the C-in-C, Mediterranean. Prior to taking over the *Centaur* he had commanded the Colossus-class light fleet carrier HMS *Triumph* for her last commission before she became a cadet training ship.

One Fleet Air Arm rating who joined the ship in September 1953 was Michael Coles, who recalls the occasion thus: 'I travelled from Culdrose to Chatham where the advance parties were assembled. After an overnight stay in Chatham Barracks we left by train for Heysham and a night crossing of the Irish Sea to the *Centaur* at Belfast, where we were welcomed on board with a full breakfast. I can remember that we were all very impressed when we found bunks in the mess decks and the cafeteria system, with a dining hall. Unfortunately there was a problem with the bunks in that they were shorter than our hammock mattresses which we had brought with us, but eventually we got new mattresses which were the correct size.'

The *Centaur* was commissioned for the first time at noon on Thursday 17 September 1953, and over the next two days 580 members of the ship's company joined her. On Sunday 20 September, after morning prayers in the hangar, Captain Sears addressed his new ship's company and that same afternoon the ship was opened to relatives and other guests. Next day preparations started in earnest to prepare *Centaur* for sea, and at 8.10am on Tuesday 22 September the mooring ropes were slipped and tugs towed her clear of Harland & Wolff's yard towards the buoyed channel of Belfast Lough and the open sea. Although she was under the command of Captain Sears with his ship's company on board, she was flying the Red Ensign and all the navigating was carried out under the direction of Captain McLaren, Harland & Wolff's trials master. By 11am she had reached the open sea where she underwent a two-hour trial of the main engines at 44,700 SHP, before working up to full power for seven hours as she steamed south off the Irish coast. At 8.20pm the full-power trial was successfully concluded and ten minutes later, in a position Lat 50° - 40'N/Long 05° - 20'W, just north of Newquay, Captain Sears accepted HMS *Centaur* into the Royal Navy and the White Ensign was broken at the masthead for the first time.

At just before midnight on that same evening the *Centaur* anchored in Bangor Bay and all the Harland & Wolff employees were disembarked into tenders to return to their homes. Next day an official reception was held on board for the directors of the Belfast shipbuilding company before, on Thursday 24 September 1953, the *Centaur* weighed anchor to start the first of four days of trials which also provided a familiarization period for her ship's company, enabling them to get to know their new ship.

It is interesting to note that the *Centaur*, as the first of the class to have left the builder's yard, was the only one to have been completed to the original design with an axial flight deck, with just one broken white line running down the centre of the deck, from forward to aft. Both the *Albion* and *Bulwark* remained at their respective builder's yards for another eight and 13 months, and when they emerged, the 5½° angled flight decks had been incorporated into their construction. Fortunately, the *Centaur* would not have long to wait before she was also modified, becoming in the process the first of the Royal Navy's aircraft carriers in service with an angled flight deck. The total cost of her building amounted to £7,906,044.00.

Chapter Two

First Commission – A New Look

During the evening of Monday 28 September 1953 the *Centaur* weighed anchor and set course for Spithead, and during the passage furnace fuel oil (FFO) consumption trials were carried out. She arrived in St Helens Roads off the Isle of Wight on the morning of Wednesday 30 September, and after spending the following day at anchor she made her first entry into Portsmouth Harbour during the afternoon of Friday 2 October, being secured alongside North Corner Jetty at 3pm. Plans were well advanced to take the *Centaur* into Portsmouth Dockyard in order to fit a 5½° 'interim' angled flight deck, but first she was scheduled to undergo a series of trials in the Channel. These started on the morning of Tuesday 6 October, when the *Centaur* made her first ceremonial departure from Portsmouth with her flight deck fully manned. There then followed ten days of machinery trials during which the *Centaur* would anchor at Spithead each evening just before dusk. On completion

of these she re-entered Portsmouth Harbour on the morning of Friday 16 October and berthed alongside North Corner Jetty where 'Finished With Engines' was rung on the engine room telegraphs. The *Centaur* was to remain in dockyard hands for the next six months.

During the three weeks she spent at North Corner Jetty, catapult deadload trials were carried out and then on Thursday 5 November she was towed into No 3 basin so that work could commence on cutting down the port sheerstrake and resiting the port walkways and the port forward bofors, together with their directors, as the flight deck was extended. Despite the extensive alterations being carried out, there was a constant stream of visitors to the *Centaur*, including the C-in-C Home Fleet, Admiral Sir Michael Denny KCB CBE DSO, as well as several senior officers from the *Albion*, which was in the final stages of her construction on the River Tyne. On the last day of December 1953, with the interior of the ship resembling

With her new angled flight deck and looking very smart as her ship's company man the flight deck, the *Centaur* leaves Portsmouth at just before midday on Monday 26 April 1954.   (*D. Palmer*)

The *Centaur* at anchor in St Helens Roads.

(D. Palmer)

the same chaotic state of her time spent at the builder's yard, Boy Seaman J. Bailey, the youngest member of the ship's company, rang 16 bells to herald in the new year.

During the first few weeks of 1954 the *Centaur's* flight deck became cluttered with all sorts of paraphernalia as it took on the appearance of a main road under repair, rather than an 'airstrip'. However, from this confusion of tools and building materials, boxes and benches, emerged the new $5^1/_2°$ angled flight deck and by March 1954 the work was nearing completion, with the result that some semblance of order was restored on board. That month the ship's chapel, St Christopher's Church, was dedicated by the Chaplain of the Fleet, and in early April the BBC broadcast a light entertainment programme from C hangar. Finally, with the angled deck completed, the *Centaur* was moored in Fareham Creek where the ship's company were employed for the next nine days cleaning up ready for her first official visit and in preparation for her flying trials. On 22 April the *Centaur* moved alongside Pitch House Jetty and four days later she left Portsmouth Harbour for St Helens Roads, where she remained at anchor for three days until 4.30pm on Thursday 29 April, when she set course up the Channel for Sheerness. As the *Centaur* was a Chatham ship, this was the closest she could get to her manning port and by midday on the last day of April she was secured to No 2 buoy at Sheerness. Despite the fact that she was lying almost a mile offshore, the ten-day visit

to the port was a great success, with civic dignitaries from both Sheerness and Chatham being entertained on board, and two open days which were well attended by the residents of the Medway towns and even attracted sightseeing pleasure boats from Southend and the Thames.

The *Centaur's* visit to Sheerness ended on the afternoon of Monday 10 May when, at 4pm, she made a ceremonial departure for Weymouth and two more days of trials. Once these were completed she returned to Spithead during the late afternoon of Thursday 13 May, where ships of the Home Fleet were assembling to welcome HMY *Britannia* and Her Majesty The Queen on her return to the United Kingdom after the Royal Tour, most of which had been undertaken on board the Shaw Savill liner, *Gothic*.

The Royal Tour had started almost six months earlier in late November 1953, when the Queen and Prince Philip left London by air for Newfoundland and Bermuda before joining the *Gothic* at Kingston, Jamaica. The liner then steamed west through the Panama Canal and on to Australia and New Zealand via a number of Pacific Islands. From Fremantle the *Gothic* set course for Colombo where the royal visitors stayed for eleven days before crossing the Arabian Sea for the Crown Colony of Aden, where the Queen and Prince Philip left the *Gothic* to continue their tour of East Africa by air. In the meantime, on Wednesday 14 April 1954, the brand new Royal Yacht *Britannia* (Captain J. S. Dalglish RN) left Portsmouth for Malta with

The *Centaur's* new angled flight deck. She was the first British aircraft carrier to be fitted with the angled deck.

(Fleet Air Arm Museum)

The first helicopter, a Dragonfly, lands on the flight deck whilst the ship is anchored off St Helens Roads, Isle of Wight, on Thursday 29 April 1954.
(D. Palmer)

Prince Charles and Princess Anne on board. After waiting in Malta, the *Britannia* steamed south to Tobruk where, on 30 April, the Queen and Prince Philip embarked and were reunited with their children. In those days the government of Libya was in the hands of King Idris who was sympathetic to the West, and there was even a British military base in the country at El Adem near Tobruk.

After leaving the Libyan port the *Britannia* returned to Malta where she was given a ceremonial welcome by naval units of the Mediterranean Fleet, including the fleet carrier HMS *Eagle*. On Friday 7 May the royal party left Malta on board *Britannia* and after calling at Gibraltar three days later, courses were set for London. However, elaborate arrangements had been made for the homecoming and on the morning of Friday 14 May 1954 the *Britannia* was met by warships of the Home Fleet, led by the battleship HMS *Vanguard* flying the flag of the C-in-C Home Fleet, Admiral Sir Michael Denny KCB CBE DSO. The rendezvous took place seven miles south-east of Eddystone Light and as the first rounds of the royal salute were fired by the *Vanguard*, the morning mist cleared and the sun broke through to give a lovely clear day. The Home Fleet ships wheeled at 180° with *Vanguard* passing close under the Royal Yacht's stern, to take up station with HM ships *Glasgow*, *Saintes* and *Barfleur*, which had escorted the *Britannia* from Gibraltar.

For the rest of the day the Royal Yacht steamed along the south coast and at 11am she met the aircraft carrier HMS *Triumph*, flying the flag of Admiral Sir Alexander Madden, the C-in-C Plymouth. Also on board HMS *Triumph* were 300 naval cadets and trainees who joined with the ship's company to man the flight deck and cheer ship as the *Triumph* steamed past. At 4pm, as the *Britannia* and her escorts passed four miles south of Portland Bill, the aircraft carriers of the Home Fleet Training Squadron, *Implacable* and *Indefatigable*, steamed past and cheered ship.

By 5.30pm the *Britannia* was off The Needles and the Home Fleet escort, except HMS *Duchess*, handed over their task to the destroyer *Grenville* and a squadron of fast patrol boats. Soon afterwards the Royal Yacht passed through the Needles Channel into the waters of the Solent where, at Spithead, the *Centaur* and ships from the Portsmouth Command had assembled. As she steamed through the Solent, 60 Wyverns, Sea Hawks and Sea Venoms of the Fleet Air Arm provided a fly-past and the coastguard station flew 'Welcome Home' signal flags.

Shortly after 7pm the Royal Yacht approached the lines of warships which were anchored at Spithead, dressed overall and with their ships' companies manning the upper decks. Despite the fact that a mist was beginning to fall, it was a splendid sight. It was the *Centaur's* duty to fire the royal salute of 21 guns, and as the *Britannia* passed by, the ship's company gave three hearty cheers, while the bells of Portsmouth Cathedral rang out and a further salute was

The *Centaur* at anchor off the Isle of Wight on 29 April 1954, shortly before she left for Sheerness.

(Fleet Air Arm Museum)

fired from the cannon at Southsea Castle.

By 8pm the *Britannia* had passed the Nab Tower and was heading up Channel, and half an hour later the *Centaur* weighed anchor and set course for Lyme Bay where she was to carry out machinery and radar trials. These lasted for five days and after spending the weekend of 22 and 23 May at anchor in Spithead, where an Avenger was embarked by lighter, she left on the morning of 24 May to begin her flying trials in the Channel. At 1.40pm that day the recently embarked Avenger was launched, the first of the fixed-wing aircraft to take off, and Michael Coles recalls the event: 'Eventually the great day came when we started our deck landing trials and the commander spoke to us over the tannoy before they started. He said the USS *Antietam* had carried out 1,500 deck landings without a single accident and that we could beat that figure. The first launch was carried out by Captain Sears in an Avenger, but that same afternoon we had our first accident when a Sea Fury crashed whilst landing. We then spent the rest of the day painting a broad yellow stripe down the port side of the deck, in line with the angle.'

Next day, after carrying out a replenishment at sea (RAS) exercise with the planeguard destroyer HMS *Obdurate*, the first Sea Hawks from RNAS Ford landed on and for the following three days deck landing trials were successfully carried out without any accidents. However, at 11.50 am on Saturday 29 May, while Sea Furies of 810 Squadron were carrying out deck landing practice south of the Isle of Wight, one of the planes crashed over the ship's bow on landing. The aircraft in question, which was piloted by Lieutenant C. J. Scott RN, had failed to pick up any of the wires with its arrester hook. Although a white flag was waved to him from the starboard side of the flight deck abreast of the island - which was an indication to a pilot that he had missed the wires - Lieutenant Scott was slow to realize what had happened and he was late opening the throttle. However, he then opened it very rapidly and with the nose of the aircraft fairly high, he stalled the engine just clear of the flight deck on the port side forward, just abreast of the after end of the port catapult, and crashed into the sea. Fortunately, Lieutenant Scott was rescued by *Obdurate's* seaboat on this occasion, but he would not be so lucky when, shortly afterwards, he was involved in another accident. That afternoon, as *Centaur* returned to her Spithead anchorage, she passed HMS *Eagle* flying the flag of Rear-Admiral W. T. Couchman, Flag Officer Heavy Squadron, while she performed a series of 'Shop Window' exercises. After saluting the flag of FOHS, the *Centaur* anchored at Spithead where the trials officers and personnel disembarked. Following a weekend at anchor, the first two days of June were spent in the Channel carrying out gunnery exercises, before *Centaur* returned to Portsmouth and secured alongside Pitch House

(Fleet Air Arm Museum)

The *Centaur* at anchor off the Isle of Wight on 29 April 1954, shortly before she left for Sheerness.

The *Centaur* at Spithead during the evening of Friday 14 May 1954, when she was part of the Review Fleet which welcomed home the Queen and Prince Philip from their Commonwealth Tour.
(D. Palmer)

During her trials in the Channel the *Centaur* carries out a replenishment at sea (RAS) exercise with the destroyer HMS *Obdurate*.
(D. Palmer)

Full-power trials in Weymouth Bay during May 1954.
(D. Palmer & H. C. Edwards)

During her flying trials in May 1954 an unserviceable Firebrand meets a watery grave.
(D. Palmer)

The *Centaur* leaves Portsmouth during the afternoon of Monday 19 July 1954, a gloriously sunny day, to prepare for her commissioning ceremony at Spithead. *(D. Palmer)*

HRH The Duchess of Kent takes the salute as the ship's company march past her dias abaft the after lift. *(D. Palmer)*

Jetty at 3.30pm on Wednesday 2 June 1954, and the ship's company were able to take foreign service leave.

At the end of June the *Centaur* was joined at Portsmouth by her newly commissioned sister ship *Albion*. It was intended that both carriers would serve for a time with the Mediterranean Fleet during their first commissions but, with the *Centaur* due to arrive on station at the end of July, it would be some weeks before the two ships would operate together as part of the fleet. The *Centaur* was scheduled to spend some time in the Mediterranean and then in late November 1954 relieve

HMS *Warrior* on the Far East Station where, despite the armistice agreement of 27 July 1953, the United Nations were continuing to station forces in South Korea.

On Tuesday 13 July 1954, after shifting her berth from C Lock to South Railway Jetty, the advance parties of 806 (Sea Hawk) Squadron, 810 (Sea Fury) Squadron and 820 (Avenger) Squadron, embarked. Six days later, at 2.30pm on Monday 19 July, a gloriously sunny day, the *Centaur* left Portsmouth Harbour and steamed past the crowds on Southsea seafront to anchor at Spithead. Next morning, after weighing anchor at 7.30am, the Sea Hawks, Avengers and Sea Furies were landed on safely, before she again anchored at Spithead where preparations were made for the arrival of her royal sponsor, HRH The Duchess of Kent, who was to attend a service of dedication on board.

The morning of Wednesday 21 July 1954 dawned dull and cheerless, but by 9am the sun had broken through and a glorious warm and sunny day followed. At 11.20am the sound of a royal salute from Portsmouth Dockyard heralded the approach of the C-in-C's barge, which was wearing the personal standard of the Duchess of Kent, and at 11.40am, accompanied by the C-in-C Portsmouth, Admiral Sir John H. Edelston GCB GCVO CBE, the *Centaur's* royal sponsor was received aboard by Captain Sears and Commander C. P. Norman DSO DSC RN, the carrier's Executive Officer. From the quarterdeck the Duchess of Kent was conducted by way of the after aircraft lift to the flight deck where she was awaited by a guard of the Royal Marines and the ship's company at Divisions.

After receiving a royal salute and inspecting the guard of honour, Her Royal Highness then went to a dias abaft the after lift to take the salute at the march past by the assembled Divisions. Following the march past, Divisions were re-formed in the shape of a 'U' around a second dias abreast the

carrier's island superstructure to which the Duchess of Kent had moved after Captain Sears had presented the Heads of Department to her. From here the Chaplain of the Fleet conducted a short service, calling for the blessing of the ship and all who served in her. After the hymn, 'Eternal Father', Captain Sears read the lesson from Psalm 107 beginning, 'They that go down to the sea in ships', and this was followed by the prayer for the Royal Navy. Finally the Chaplain of the Fleet pronounced the blessing of the ship, following which Divisions were dispersed.

After the service the Duchess went to the ante-room to meet the officers from both the ship and the squadrons, and afterwards she had lunch with them in the wardroom. During the afternoon the royal visitor toured the ship where she saw the church, the sick bay, the dining halls, a CPOs mess, where the tiered bunks were laid out for inspection, and finally, the hangar. At 2.15pm, after a royal salute and the playing of the National Anthem, the Duchess of Kent, accompanied by the C-in-C, made her departure.

Later that afternoon, at 4pm, the *Centaur* weighed anchor and steamed into the Channel for four days of flying exercises in the Lyme Bay area before sailing for the Mediterranean.

The short Commissioning Service was held on the flight deck abreast of the island superstructure. On the dias from left to right are HRH The Duchess of Kent, The Chaplain of the Fleet and Captain H. P. Sears RN.   *(D. Palmer)*

Chapter Three

First Commission – Mediterranean Fleet

After completing the first phase of her flying trials the *Centaur* left home waters on Monday 26 July 1954 and set course for Gibraltar, where she arrived four days later and secured alongside 47 berth on the South Mole. She was scheduled to spend four months in the Mediterranean, before making a southbound transit of the Suez Canal to relieve HMS *Warrior* in the Far East. It was on Friday 6 August 1954, when she made a ceremonial entry into Malta's Grand Harbour and fired a 17-gun salute to the C-in-C Mediterranean Fleet, Admiral The Earl Mountbatten of Burma, that she formally joined the Mediterranean Station. Three days later she steamed out of the harbour to the Libyan coast to carry out the next phase of her flying trials. Sadly this was marred on Thursday 12 August by the ship's first fatal flying accident which happened when the *Centaur* was just north of the port of Tripoli. That afternoon the flying programme consisted of

a serial of two Sea Hawks, which were launched by catapult, followed by three Avengers and three Sea Furies which were to make free take-offs from the flight deck. The wind speed required was 22 knots, and to achieve this with a natural wind of 12 knots the ship steamed at $16^1/_2$ knots and the two Sea Hawks were launched successfully. The piston-engined aircraft were then ranged and launched at 20-second intervals, with a slightly longer pause between the last Avenger and the first Sea Fury, which was piloted by Lieutenant C. J. Scott RN. After the last Avenger was safely away it was the turn of Lt Scott, and the circumstances were later described by Captain Sears in his evidence to the subsequent Inquiry: 'As he (Lt Scott) came past the compass platform the engine sounded absolutely normal at full throttle. It is true that I keep the windows of the compass platform closed to reduce the noise of the jets, but I have no hesitation in making that

The *Centaur* arrives in Grand Harbour for the first time on Friday 6 August 1954. The cruiser HMS *Gambia* is moored astern.

(H. C. Edwards)

On 12 August 1954, during flying operations off Tripoli, the *Centaur's* first fatal accident took place when a Sea Fury crashed into the sea after it had been launched.
(Fleet Air Arm Museum)

statement. He was comfortably airborne as he left the end of the deck and he started a turn to starboard, allowing the nose of the aircraft to rise, assuming therefore the position of a climbing turn. To my astonishment the turn was allowed to steepen and without any apparent correction for bank or height of the nose, the aircraft continued to bank right over, the nose came down and the aircraft, still at full throttle, went into the sea. Immediately I put the wheel hard to starboard and went astern on both engines, and the ship drew up a cable and a half from the point where the aircraft entered the water and to windward of that position. A seaboat was lowered and the helicopter was at the scene of the accident in a matter of seconds. Unfortunately, although the search was maintained by the helicopter and the motor cutter for about an hour, no trace of Lieutenant Scott was seen. The motor cutter and the helicopter were left at the scene of the crash whilst the ship proceeded to recover the aircraft which were airborne, and on return from this operation, which was about an hour after the crash, the cutter was rehoisted, helicopter embarked and the search abandoned.' The Inquiry found that the cause of the accident was, '... either a failure of the pilot to realize that the aircraft was assuming an uncontrollable nose up attitude after his take-off or, realizing this, he was too slow in taking the correct recovery action.'

On 8 October 1954 the *Centaur*, together with 20 other units of the Mediterranean Fleet, took part in a programme of exercises and manoeuvres in honour of Emperor Haile Selassie of Ethiopia. In this view the ship's company man the flight deck as the Emperor passes by on board HMS *Gambia*.
(D. Palmer)

Lord Mountbatten and other senior NATO officers watch flying operations at sea on 2 September 1954.

(R. F. Bennett)

The remainder of the trials were completed without serious incident and on Thursday 2 September the *Centaur* stopped 600 yards from the entrance to Grand Harbour to embark Lord Mountbatten and other senior officers for a day at sea during which the ship and the three squadrons were successfully put through their paces. During the visit Lord Mountbatten announced to the ship's company that *Centaur* would not, after all, be joining the Far East Fleet, but instead she would remain with the Mediterranean Fleet and would be employed on a special duty which would be very different from her role as a strike carrier. The return of the *Warrior* to the UK following the decision to reduce the numbers of United Nations forces in Korea meant that for the first time since the end of the Second World War there would be no operational British aircraft carrier on the Far East Station. According to Michael Coles, this policy was not popular with a large number of the ship's company who had been looking forward to a stint 'east of Suez'. It meant also that the *Centaur* would remain based on Malta until the

summer of 1955 when she would return to the UK for the NATO autumn exercises in the grey waters of the North Sea, rather than in the 'spiced tropical waters' of South-East Asia.

However, prior to her special mission, the *Centaur* took part in fleet manoeuvres in the exercise areas off Malta with the destroyer *Chevron* and the Daring-class destroyers *Diamond, Diana, Duchess* and *Decoy*. It was during these exercises, at 4.35am on the morning of Saturday 2 October 1954, that the *Chevron* collided with the *Centaur's* port side causing slight damage to the upperworks of both ships but, fortunately, no casualties. The two vessels were able to continue the exercises, during which they anchored in Marsaxlokk Bay each evening.

On Friday 8 October 1954 the *Centaur*, together with 20 other units of the Mediterranean Fleet, took part in a programme of exercises and manoeuvres in honour of His Imperial Majesty Haile Selassie I, the Emperor of Ethiopia, who, apart from a five-year break between 1936 and 1941, had ruled Ethiopia since 1930. He was the son of the chief advisor to Emperor Menelik II and he was born in 1892 as Ras (Prince) Tafari Makonnen, (the inspiration for the Rastafarian cult). In 1917, when Menelik's daughter became Empress, Ras Tafari was appointed regent and heir apparent and he was very much associated with the movement for modernization and reform in his country. In 1923 it was he who negotiated Ethiopia's membership of the League of Nations and, in November 1930, on the death of Empress Zauditu, he was crowned Emperor Haile Selassie I, which means 'Might of the Trinity'. He quickly established a personal autocracy in Ethiopia, but he also took positive steps towards modernizing the country. In 1935, when Italy invaded Ethiopia, (Abyssinia as it was known then), having set himself up in the position of 'warrior-emperor', he took up arms against the invaders. June 1936 saw the fall of Addis Ababa to the Italian Army, whereupon Haile Selassie was forced to flee, and he was taken out of the country in the cruiser HMS *Capetown* although, on arrival at Gibraltar, he was transferred to the Orient Line passenger ship *Orford*, which was a political move by the British Government. During his period of exile he based himself in London and in May 1941, following General Sir Lewis Heath's successful campaign in Eritrea, Somaliland and Ethiopia, which drove out the Italian Army, Haile Selassie was restored to his throne. He then set about rebuilding his former autocracy which led to a great deal of internal resentment in the years following the end of the Second World War. However, he was also dedicated to emphasizing his country's prominence in the late 1940s and early 1950s as one of the few countries on the continent of Africa which was independent of European colonial control. It can be seen, therefore, that given this background the Emperor was a very loyal British ally and in the atmosphere of those 'Cold War' days, such friendships were highly regarded in the West. This was

The *Centaur* in Grand Harbour during 1954, as seen from her sister ship, HMS *Albion*. *(Lt-Cdr H. Lyons)*

Centaur leaves Grand Harbour, during her first commission.   *(Lt-Cdr H. Lyons)*

The ceremonial steam past for Emperor Haile Selassie by ships of the Mediterranean Fleet, which took place on 8 October 1954.

(D. Palmer)

Soldiers embarking at Trieste at the end of October 1954, while members of the ship's company, who seem to be enjoying a tea break, look on.

(H. C. Edwards)

The evacuation of troops from Trieste at the end of October 1954. Men of the Lancashire Regiment parade on the quayside before embarking in the *Centaur*.
(*R. F. Bennett*)

The return to Grand Harbour on 28 October 1954 with all the troops and their vehicles after the evacuation from Trieste.

(D. Palmer & H. C. Edwards)

reflected in the sophisticated manoeuvres which were organized for the occasion, with four Pakistani destroyers also involved, all of them ex-Royal Navy vessels, including the *Taimur* which only nine weeks previously had been HMS *Chivalrous*. Also present was a Royal Australian Air Force wing to participate in a fly-past.

For the *Centaur* and other units of the fleet the day started at 8am when they left the anchorage at Marsaxlokk Bay in grey, wet and windy conditions, and an hour later the cruiser *Gambia*, wearing the standard of Emperor Haile Selassie and escorted by the C-in-C's dispatch vessel, HMS

Surprise, left Grand Harbour to the crash of a royal salute from the shore batteries. The *Gambia* rendezvoused with the fleet, which included the cruiser *Glasgow*, wearing the flag of Admiral Mountbatten, and the cruiser *Bermuda*, flying the flag of Vice-Admiral J. P. L. Reid, Flag Officer Second in Command Mediterranean Fleet. There then followed a fly-past by jet aircraft of the Fleet Air Arm and the RAAF, and by helicopters of the Fleet Air Arm, before the real demonstration commenced. This began with a 6-inch shoot by *Glasgow* and *Bermuda* firing against the *Gambia*, followed by a torpedo attack by all the destroyers and frigates firing dummy torpedoes across the *Gambia's* bows. The four Daring-class destroyers, *Duchess*, *Diana*, *Diamond* and *Decoy*, then carried out an anti-submarine mortar attack off the *Gambia's* starboard bow, before it was the *Centaur's* turn to demonstrate catapult launchings and landings by the Sea Hawks of 801 Squadron. The finale came at 11.30 am when the fleet performed a ceremonial steam-past, with all the ships fully manned and each ship's company giving three cheers. At just before 1pm the manoeuvres ended when the *Gambia* left the fleet to return to the UK. Haile Selassie survived as the leader of Ethiopia, despite an attempted coup in 1960, until September 1974 when he was overthrown by middle-ranking army officers. He died less than a year later on 27 August 1975, in unexplained circumstances.

Following all the great effort put into the work-up and the fleet manoeuvres for the Emperor of Ethiopia, the *Centaur's* ship's company were now to be allowed some relaxation in the form of a four-day visit to Naples, where they arrived at just before noon on Saturday 9 October. The visit ended early on Wednesday 13 October, and by the following morning *Centaur* had arrived back in Malta's

Grand Harbour and was secured alongside Parlatorio Wharf to carry out a week of self-maintenance. During the stay, on the morning of Saturday 16 October, Captain Henry C. Rolfe RN joined the ship and on the next day he assumed command of HMS *Centaur* from Captain Sears, who left for the UK and his well-earned retirement. Captain Rolfe had joined the Navy in 1925 and during the Second World War he served in the ill-fated carrier HMS *Hermes* and with South-East Asia Command, based at Trincomalee in Ceylon (Sri Lanka). After the war he commanded the frigate *Veryan Bay*, the aircraft carrier HMS *Vengeance*, and RNAS Culdrose in Cornwall. Two days after the change of command, the *Centaur's* sister ship, HMS *Albion*, entered Grand Harbour for the first time as she too joined the Mediterranean Fleet, having just completed her trials and work-up. However, before the two carriers could operate together, the *Centaur* had to carry out the rather unusual duty of evacuating British troops from the city of Trieste, and she left Malta during the afternoon of Thursday 21 October with the destroyers *Roebuck* and *Whirlwind* to steam across the Adriatic Sea to the ancient Roman port, where she berthed, port side to,

Heavy weather in the Mediterranean.

(D. Palmer)

Flying is completed for the day and the *Centaur* is anchored off Marsaxlokk.   *(R. F. Bennett)*

Twin sisters? The *Centaur* (right) and *Albion* at Toulon, January 1955.   *(Fleet Air Arm Museum)*

During the morning of 24 March 1955, HRH The Duke of Edinburgh paid a visit to the *Centaur* whilst she was at sea. Here he transfers by jackstay from the *Britannia*.

(G. Morter)

on the south side of Mole 6 at 8.50am on Sunday 24 October.

Before the Great War of 1914-18 Trieste had been a prosperous city and the major port of the Austro-Hungarian Empire, and the end of the war in 1918 made an immense difference to Italy which, of course, had fought on the Allied side. Italy acquired a large part of the northern Adriatic coast in the former Hapsburg Empire, including the ancient city port of Trieste and 213 merchant ships which had once sailed under the Austro-Hungarian flag. The Treaty of St-Germain, which obliged Austria to recognize the independence of Yugoslavia - the kingdom of Serbs, Croats and Slovenes which had been proclaimed by Prince Alexander on 4 December 1918 - confirmed Italy's new acquisitions. The consequences of these upheavals which followed the Great War are still being felt in Europe today and, once again in the 1990s, the Royal Navy has played its part in international efforts to resolve the current political problems. During the Second World War, with Italy this time on the side of the Axis forces, the liberation of the northern Adriatic coast was carried out by New Zealand troops, but Trieste was actually occupied first by President Tito's Yugoslavian partisans and the city became a source of dispute between the government of the newly formed Italian republic and Tito, who felt that as the heir to the Balkan territories which had once formed part of the Austro-Hungarian Empire, Yugoslavia was entitled to this important city and port. As part of the formal peace treaty of February 1947, where Italy was called on to pay the price of Mussolini's alliance with Hitler and where she lost territory which had been ceded at the end of the Great War, the Trieste Free Territory was declared as a compromise, with Zone A being occupied by American and British troops under the auspices of the United Nations, and Zone B being occupied by Yugoslavia. Under the terms of the Italian peace treaty Trieste was supposed to have been an independent state under the supervision of the United Nations, but terms between the Western powers and Tito's government could not be agreed and finally, on 8 October 1954, the USA and Britain announced that they were withdrawing their troops from Zone A and handing over control to the Italians, who were already policing the zone. As Zone A comprised most of Trieste, President Tito was furious at this move and crowds of protesters in Belgrade smashed windows at the US, British and Italian Embassies. This was the background to events which brought the *Centaur* to the port, and it took two days to embark the British troops and their equipment in the carrier, filling the hangar to capacity with armoured vehicles and camp beds. Finally, with the embarkation complete, the *Centaur* slipped her mooring ropes at 9am on Tuesday 26 October and left the Adriatic port with her unusual passengers. Just over 48 hours later she was once again alongside Parlatorio Wharf in Grand Harbour and disembarkation began.

During November the *Centaur* took part in exercises with the *Albion* which, according to Michael Coles, soon became known to the flight deck personnel as the 'heap'. He remembers that during the exercises 'Little F' (Lieutenant-Commander Flying), '...came over the flight deck tannoy to tell us to get a move on or he would crack the whip. He also said that the "heap", meaning the *Albion*, was watching us and that we, the "wallflower" must beat her. After that *Albion* was always referred to as the "heap" and we became the "wallflower". We actually presented "Little F" with a whip.'

The *Centaur* spent most of the first two weeks of December at sea in the naval exercise areas off Malta and off the coast of Tripoli with *Albion* and other units of the Mediterranean Fleet but, to everyone's relief, on Wednesday 15 December 1954 she secured alongside Parlatorio Wharf in Grand Harbour for a stay of just over

The Duke of Edinburgh visits the galley during his tour of the *Centaur*.

(H. C. Edwards)

four weeks, which included Christmas and the New Year. During this time Rear-Admiral Couchman, the FOAC, struck his flag and his successor, Rear-Admiral A. R. Pedder, hoisted his flag in the *Centaur*.

It was on Wednesday 12 January 1955 that the *Centaur* put to sea once again and after a week of intensive flying, which included a display for the Governor of Malta, she and the *Albion* made a four-day visit to Toulon. The two sisters berthed alongside No 5 Jetty in the French naval base and both proved very popular with the local residents on open days. Following the visit both the *Centaur* and *Albion* took part in joint exercises with the US Navy's Sixth Fleet, including the carriers *Randolph* and *Lake Champlain*, the battleship *Iowa* (wearing the flag of Rear-Admiral E. Libby USN), and the command ship *Northampton* (Vice-Admiral T. S. Combs USN). On the first day of the manoeuvres air defence exercises were carried out, and on Sunday 30 January members of *Centaur's* ship's company made exchange visits by helicopter with the USS *Randolph*. The exercises ended on the last day of January when, to mark the occasion, *Centaur's* Sea Furies performed a fly-past over the Sixth Fleet, and on the next day the C-in-C Mediterranean paid a two-hour visit to the *Centaur* by helicopter. On 2 February the carrier ran into a severe westerly storm with wind speeds of over 48 knots and huge

waves which took on a white appearance as the foam was blown in dense streaks. Rear-Admiral Rolfe remembers Wednesday 2 February when, 'We were weather-bound off Malta riding out the storm. One of my main engines was ineffective and I was hard put to ride out the storm. However, all went well and next day the ship was able to enter Grand Harbour.'

For the remainder of February and for the first two weeks of March the *Centaur* spent a great deal of time at sea and during that period took part in 'Exercise Sea Lance' together with the *Albion* and 50 other units of the Mediterranean and Home Fleets, including the Royal Yacht *Britannia*. It was one of the largest exercises to be carried out by the Royal Navy since the end of the Second World War, and as well as involving the landing of Royal Marines by helicopter, it also tested measures designed to protect shipping and safeguard sea communications. A task force led by the cruiser *Glasgow*, flying the flag of the C-in-C Mediterranean, Admiral Sir Guy Grantham, escorted a convoy for which the *Britannia*, with the Duke of Edinburgh embarked, acted as commodore. The exercise also involved a simulated atomic explosion, the smoke for which was provided by the *Apollo* and after which all ships could test their pre-wetting systems and anti-nuclear precautions. In this situation the engine room staff had to

The two sisters, *Centaur* and *Albion* (astern), exercising together in the Mediterranean.

(Fleet Air Arm Museum)

The *Albion* in line astern of *Centaur* during Mediterranean exercises. *(D. Palmer)*

provide their ships with full power with all ventilation shut off. At the end of the exercise the *Britannia* led the fleet into Grand Harbour, where the Duke of Edinburgh was due to open Malta's new Parliament. During the exercise the *Centaur* received visits from a number of senior officers, including the First Sea Lord, Admiral Sir Rhoderick McGrigor, who arrived by helicopter and departed to HMS *Daring* by jackstay.

On Tuesday 22 March the *Centaur* and the rest of the fleet left Malta to act as escort to the Royal Yacht which was bound for Gibraltar. During the passage they were joined by the Dutch aircraft carrier *Karel Doorman* (ex-HMS *Venerable* and now the Argentine *Vienticinco De Mayo*), and the French carrier *Lafayette* (ex-USS *Langley*). At 9.10am on Thursday 24 March the Duke of Edinburgh transferred to the *Centaur* by jackstay for a visit of just over two hours, before leaving by helicopter. After the visit he sent the following message to FOAC in *Centaur*: 'I am delighted to have had the chance of visiting *Centaur* and *Albion*. I was most impressed with everything I saw, especially by the skill, efficiency and spirit of officers and men in all departments. I would like to thank you and all concerned for arranging the visits and showing me around. Philip.'

After spending three days at Gibraltar the *Centaur* left for the French town of Beaulieu-sur-Mer, which lies

between Villefranche and Monte Carlo. Despite the visit almost having to be cut short by severe gales, it was a great success and few of the ship's company had any money left when the *Centaur* left for Malta on 4 April! Following her arrival alongside Parlatorio Wharf the ship underwent a three-week self-maintenance period, which was followed by a long weekend visit to Augusta, Sicily. During May the *Centaur* spent a great deal of time rehearsing a flying display which was to be laid on for visitors from a number of Defence Colleges on the ship's return to UK waters during the following month, and on the last day of May she secured alongside 47 berth on Gibraltar's South Mole. By now everyone on board was looking forward to returning home and there were sighs of relief when, at 9.30am on Thursday 2 June, *Centaur* left Gibraltar and set course for Portsmouth. On the evening of Sunday 5 June she anchored in Lyme Bay for the night and next morning the squadrons were flown off to their respective stations. That same evening the *Centaur* anchored at Spithead to wait for customs clearance and, unusually, clearance from government veterinary inspectors. During the *Centaur's* eleven months in the Mediterranean many of the ship's company had bought budgerigars as pets, and when CERA Richard Coleman fell ill during the passage home it was thought that he was suffering from a disease which can be contracted from these birds. And so, on the morning of Tuesday 7 June, all ratings who had purchased budgies were summoned to present their pets in the hangar for a veterinary check, an operation which caused some surprise amongst the senior officers when 475 owners and birds arrived for inspection. However, the story has a happy ending, for CERA Coleman was not diagnosed as having psittacosis and the *Centaur's* collection of birds were exonerated from blame. That same afternoon, at 1.50pm, the *Centaur* weighed anchor and with her flight deck fully manned she steamed up harbour to secure alongside Portsmouth Dockyard's South Railway Jetty, where hundreds of relatives and friends were waiting to greet their loved ones. Michael Coles even remembers a large banner being displayed on the jetty declaring, 'Welcome Home Wallflower'. The *Centaur's* reputation had obviously gone on ahead of her.

The first half of the *Centaur's* first commission had been a great success, even though she had not managed to leave the Mediterranean.

Clear lower deck of budgies! The return to Portsmouth on 7 June 1955 and the birds await a health check before being allowed ashore. *(D. Palmer)*

Chapter Four

First Commission – East of Suez

After a break of only six days the *Centaur* left Portsmouth again, at 10.30am on Monday 13 June 1955, this time bound for the area south-west of the Isle of Wight where she was to take part in a ten-day 'Shop Window' exercise. Other participating ships were the frigate *Grenville*, which acted as the *Centaur's* planeguard ship, the T-class submarine *Tapir*, four Fairmile D-class gunboats of the 1st Fast Patrol Boat Squadron and the four Gay-class torpedo boats of the 2nd Fast Patrol Boat Squadron.

As soon as she arrived at the designated area, Sea Hawks of 803 and 806 Squadrons were embarked, together with Avengers of 814 Squadron. For the first day of the exercises the spectators were limited to 80 cadets of the Combined Cadet Force who were able to enjoy a full dress rehearsal of the programme which was to be repeated over the following days for guests from the RAF Staff College, the Imperial Defence College, the Army Staff College and the Joint Services Staff College, as well as observers from the Admiralty and even a crowned head of state. However, probably the most popular guests as far as the ship's company were concerned were 50 Wrens from the various naval barracks in the Portsmouth area.

Each day the programme would begin with a demonstration by HMS *Grenville* of the Mark 10 anti-submarine mortar which the frigate fired from the *Centaur's* starboard side. For the second serial *Grenville* would close *Centaur's* starboard side to demonstrate the light jackstay method of replenishment and transfer at sea which was, and still is, used as a quick and simple method of exchanging light stores and personnel between ships at sea. The third serial of the exercise involved the fast patrol boats carrying out a mock attack on the *Centaur*, before passing close up the starboard side of the carrier. Finally, before the lunch break, HMS *Tapir* would close to *Centaur* on the same course and when level with the carrier's island superstructure she would dive to periscope depth then, before surfacing once again, she would raise her periscope and 'snort' in order to show her position.

During the afternoon programme the *Centaur* herself became the centre of attraction when she put on her flying display, which included the launching, recovery and operational turnround of Sea Hawk and Avenger aircraft. This was followed by a fly-past of all the aircraft, and formation and solo aerobatic displays by the Sea Hawks of 806 Squadron. The Sea Hawks of both 803 and 806 Squadrons then demonstrated weapons attacks on a splash target towed by the *Centaur*. The Avengers in their turn demonstrated an anti-submarine depth charge attack. Next the *Centaur's* S51 Dragonfly helicopter undertook a

During a series of 'Shop Window' displays off the Isle of Wight during June 1955, one of the VIPs who spent a day on board was the young King Hussein of Jordan. He is seen here arriving by Dragonfly helicopter.

(G. Morter)

A series of photographs taken on 5 September 1955, when Sea Hawk N150, with its throttle stuck open, careered down the flight deck into the four other Sea Hawks parked at the forward end, scattering the flight deck personnel and knocking four men into the sea. In the third photograph of the sequence the Flight Deck Officer can be seen clinging to the plane's nose as it fell into the sea. The Hawk's tail was also sheered off in the collision and it can be seen lying next to N145. Fortunately, there were no fatalities.

(G. Morter & R. F. Bennett)

September 1955, when the *Centaur* was at Oslo with HM Ships *Eagle* and *Tyne* and HMAS *Queenborough*.
(D. Palmer)

simulated rescue at sea which, in those days, involved the use of a large 'scoop' net slung underneath the machine. The ships' fire-fighting teams then gave a demonstration of their skills, including the rescue of the crew of a crashed aircraft then, as a grand finale, the Sea Hawks of 803 Squadron carried out dummy bombing attacks on the *Centaur* while the Bofors guns' crews fired break-up shot against the 'aggressors'.

The daily programme lasted until 4.30pm and each afternoon, as the *Centaur* steamed back to her anchorage at Spithead, tea was provided for the visitors at the after end of the hangar. On Monday 20 June, as well as 70 guests from the Army Staff College at Camberley and the C-in-C Portsmouth, Admiral of the Fleet Sir George Creasy, present as guest of honour was King Hussein of Jordan who, in the mid-1950s, was perhaps Britain's closest Middle Eastern ally. King Hussein, who is now rather a controversial figure in that region, was 20 years old at the time of his visit to the *Centaur*, and he was only 18 in 1953 when he succeeded his father, who was deposed by parliament because of his mental illness. He was born in Amman, the son of King Talal, and he had been educated at Victoria College, Alexandria, before attending Harrow School and Sandhurst Military Academy. His English education encouraged him to maintain close ties with Britain and so he was a very important guest when he arrived on board by helicopter at 10.34am. During the day, the King, accompanied by the C-in-C, watched the *Centaur* and her squadrons being put through their paces. Seventeen months later, of all the Middle Eastern leaders, King Hussein would know exactly what the *Centaur's* sister ships *Albion* and *Bulwark* were capable of when their squadrons led the British and French attack on the

Egyptian airfields.

The 'Shop Window' exercises were concluded on Friday 24 June and the following day *Centaur* secured alongside Portsmouth's Middle Slip Jetty where she would undergo a nine-week refit. During July and August the ship's company were able to take their summer leave, and it was Monday 29 August when the *Centaur* left Portsmouth once again, this time bound for the North Sea and the north-east coast of Scotland. First she had to embark her squadrons, and while anchored at Spithead for two hours the next day she was joined by two Members of Parliament who were to watch the flying operations. Five days later, on Sunday 4 September, she anchored off Invergordon and before dawn on Monday she weighed anchor to start her flying operations off the Moray Firth. During the morning of 5 September there was a full flying programme until 1.30pm, which was completed without incident. However, at 2.20pm that afternoon, soon after flying operations resumed, Sea Hawk N150 piloted by Lieutenant Tisby RN landed on and, although it caught a wire on a well executed landing, just as the hook was cleared and the pilot prepared to taxi forward, the throttle stuck wide open causing the aircraft to career forward towards the deck park on the starboard side forward of the island. To the horror of the flight deck crew it went forward straight into the four other Hawks which were parked there. At the last minute the flight deck crew scattered but, like a wild rampaging beast, the Hawk crashed through the parked aircraft and carried two of the flight deck personnel overboard when it toppled over the starboard side. One of the casualties was the flight deck officer, who was left clinging to the plane's nose. As Captain Rolfe ordered 'hard-astern' to stop the ship, and the seaboat's crew were scrambled, the attendant

A Sea Hawk about to catch the wire. *(D. Palmer)*

Sunday 12 February 1956, a day of relaxation as the *Centaur* steams south through the Suez Canal. *(G. Morter)*

planeguard helicopter quickly reached the scene and its crew swept the injured FDO into their net and deposited him on the flight deck where medical attention was swiftly available. It was then the pilot's turn to be rescued and, almost simultaneously, the seaboat picked up the third man who had been knocked overboard. A muster of all the duty flight deck personnel was carried out which confirmed that everyone could be accounted for. Later that evening the *Centaur* anchored off Lossiemouth and the more seriously injured men were soon on their way to a mainland hospital. What could have been a disaster on the flight deck had been avoided and the injured had been tended quickly and efficiently. Two days later, after the *Centaur* had moored off Invergordon, the four damaged aircraft were unloaded into lighters and replacement flight deck crews joined the ship.

Later that month the *Centaur* was joined off Scotland by her sister ships *Albion* and *Bulwark*, together with the fleet carrier *Eagle* and other units of the Home Fleet, for 'Exercise Sea Enterprise' which incorporated anti-submarine manoeuvres and air strikes on the Norwegian coast. At 11.50am on Sunday 25 September, which was the penultimate day of the exercise, tragedy struck when one of the *Eagle's* Wyverns developed a serious fuel leak and attempted to make an emergency landing on the *Bulwark*. Unfortunately, the pilot was unable to make it and he crashed into the sea on the *Bulwark's* port quarter and, despite a search by SAR helicopters from both *Centaur* and *Bulwark*, there was no sign of the pilot or his aircraft. On Wednesday 28 September, on conclusion of the exercise, all four carriers and the rest of the fleet anchored in Trondheim Fjord where debriefings were held. Next day, with weather conditions having deteriorated, the *Centaur*, *Eagle*, *Apollo* (flying the flag of the C-in-C Home Fleet), *Tyne Loch Fada* and HMAS *Queenborough* weighed anchor and steamed down the Norwegian coast and through the Skagerrak to Oslo, where the *Centaur* was able to go alongside for a seven-day visit to the Norwegian capital. At this time the *Centaur* played host to Crown Prince Olav of Norway, who spent two hours on board during the evening of Thursday 6 October. It was whilst the *Centaur* was at Oslo that the Admiralty announced that she and the *Albion* were to visit the Far East Station to participate in joint tactical exercises with the Australian and New Zealand Navies. On 10 October the carriers left Oslo for Rosyth and en route they rendezvoused with the *Albion* which had been to Copenhagen. On their arrival at Rosyth they rejoined the *Bulwark* and all four carriers set about preparing for 'Exercise Phoenix I', which was intended to test the ability of the Fleet Air Arm to intercept high-level strategic bombers. At the end of the exercise the *Centaur* returned to Rosyth, where she spent four days at anchor before leaving on the afternoon of Wednesday 2 November to make a fast passage down the North Sea and the

Channel to arrive at Spithead early on 4 November. The *Albion* had, in fact, left Rosyth 24 hours before *Centaur*, but she had to await customs clearance in the Solent and so at 8.30am that morning both the *Centaur* and *Albion* entered Portsmouth Harbour together and tied up at Pitch House and Middle Slip Jetties respectively. As soon as they were safely alongside, the ships' companies of both carriers started their seasonal leave prior to the next stage of their respective commissions.

Both the *Albion* and *Centaur* left Portsmouth on the morning of Tuesday 10 January 1956, with the former flying the flag of Rear-Admiral Pedder, FOAC, and after embarking their squadrons they set course for Gibraltar, where they arrived four days later. The next few weeks were spent in the Mediterranean operating from Malta, but on Friday 10 February the *Albion* made her southbound transit of the Suez Canal with the *Centaur* following on Sunday 12 February, and the two ships met up again on 15 February, off Aden, where they commenced flying exercises with the RAF Venoms from Khormaksar. It was on the second day of the exercises, at 2.30pm on Thursday 16 February, that a Sea Hawk piloted by Lieutenant-Commander Baker RN, the commanding officer of 801 Squadron, crashed on take-off from the *Centaur's* starboard catapult. Both *Centaur's* engines were stopped immediately, the wheel was put hard-to-port and the planeguard helicopter was quickly on the scene, followed closely by the seaboat, but despite these efforts, no trace was found of the pilot or his aircraft. After searching for half an hour the *Centaur* had to get under way once again in order to recover the aircraft which had been launched prior to the accident. 'Exercise Gateway' continued over the following two days and by the morning of Friday 17 February the two carriers had arrived off the island of Socotra at the entrance to the Gulf of Aden. Two days later, in the Arabian Sea, the carriers rendezvoused with the Indian cruiser INS *Delhi* (formerly HMS *Achilles* of River Plate fame). There then followed two days of flying demonstrations, the climax of which came on Tuesday 21 February with a spectacular display by both the *Centaur* and *Albion*. This was an important exercise as the Indian Prime Minister, Mr Jawaharlal Nehru, whose government was negotiating the purchase of an aircraft carrier for the Indian Navy, was on board the *Albion* and 50 Indian Government and Defence Ministry representatives were embarked in the *Centaur* for the occasion. In the event India bought the unfinished Majestic-class aircraft carrier *Hercules*, which was eventually completed and commissioned as INS *Vikrant*. At the end of the display the visitors were transferred to the Indian Navy ships, and the *Centaur* was detached to Karachi. While en route for the port she took part in exercises with the Pakistani Navy, which involved the latter in a search for the carrier and a dummy attack by Pakistani Air Force Attackers which was

The *Centaur* alongside at Karachi, at that time the capital of Pakistan. *(M. K. Pagan)*

Sea Hawks being struck down the forward lift. *(R. F. Bennett)*

A fine view of the *Centaur* in the Indian Ocean, February 1956.

intercepted by *Centaur's* Sea Hawks. Finally, on the morning of Thursday 23 February, the *Centaur* reached Karachi which, in those days, was the capital city of Pakistan. Once again 50 government officials were embarked, including the Governor-General of Pakistan, the Commanders-in-Chief of the Pakistani Navy and Air Force and the Ministers of Defence and Finance. They were then taken out to sea where the *Centaur's* ship's company repeated the impressive display of the ship's capabilities. That afternoon the *Centaur* anchored off the port to disembark her guests and next morning she steamed into the harbour to berth alongside the West Wharf. Although the visit lasted for only three days, it was a very busy time with an official reception, a sailing regatta and an open day for the public to view the ship. This proved extremely popular with the city's residents and the local police had to turn out to 'repel boarders' among the hundreds of disappointed people who hadn't managed to get on board and who didn't think the gangway should be closed in the early evenings. The *Centaur* left Karachi at 10.15am on Monday 27 February and en route to Colombo she rendezvoused with the *Albion*, which had visited Bombay. The two ships made a fast passage south, which limited flying operations, and arrived off Colombo Harbour on the afternoon of Thursday 1 March. This call lasted for four

days and on 5 March both *Centaur* and *Albion* sailed for Singapore.

Three days later, off the Nicobar Islands, the two carriers rendezvoused with the cruiser *Sheffield* and other units of the Far East Fleet to carry out 'Exercise Welcome', which included strikes by the Sea Hawks of both *Centaur* and *Albion* on the towns of Alor Star and Butterworth and the city of Kuala Lumpur. The exercise ended with the Sea Hawks executing mock attacks on the three airfields of Tengah, Seletar and Changi on Singapore Island, followed by a fly-past over the city itself.

As the cruise to the Far East was primarily a 'flag showing' operation, on Saturday 10 March the *Centaur* anchored in the Outer Roads off Singapore city where she was floodlit in the evening, before moving round to the north coast of the island next day to secure alongside Singapore's Naval Base for a four-day stopover. Both the *Centaur* and the *Albion* left Singapore on the morning of Thursday 15 March, and after carrying out an air defence exercise in which the USAF aircraft from the Philippines acted as the attacking force over Malaya, the two carriers set course for Hong Kong where they arrived on Monday 19 March and moored to buoys in the harbour. Two days later both ships left harbour to take part in 'Exercise Sea Dragon' which involved the defence of the colony against

A Sea Hawk's oleo collapses on landing and the fire-fighting team rushes forward. *(R. F. Bennett)*

The traditional children's party was held on board during the ship's stay in Singapore during March 1956. In this view children from a local orphanage enjoy all the fun of the fair....

...followed by tea in the hangar.
(R. F. Bennett)

air attack and the provision of air support for ground troops. However, who the attackers were meant to represent was not clear for Hong Kong had always been considered by the Chiefs of Staff to be indefensible. The exercise ended on Saturday 24 March and both the *Centaur* and *Albion* returned to Hong Kong for a further two days before finally leaving on the morning of Monday 26 March for a seven-day ANZAM (Australia, New Zealand, American) exercise which would involve the air and anti-submarine defence of a convoy, and an air attack by the carrier squadrons on Singapore. Before the exercise started, aircraft from both *Centaur* and *Albion* were to participate in a farewell fly-past over Hong Kong and at 2.15pm, just five hours after leaving harbour, the first planes were launched. Unfortunately, the event was marred by tragedy when two of *Centaur's* Sea Hawks collided in mid-air and crashed near a rocky peak overlooking the eastern entrance of the harbour. Both the aircrew, Lieutenant R. A. L. Lawson RN and Lieutenant B. W. Halstone RN, were killed and a local woman also died from her injuries after the engine and a fuel tank from one of the machines fell on her house. Wreckage also landed on a nearby school, but, fortunately, it was unoccupied at the time. Despite the tragedy, both carriers left the area off

Hong Kong that day to steam into the South China Sea for 'Exercise Monsoon', in which tactics to defend vital oil tanker convoys between Singapore and Hong Kong were deployed. During the exercise *Centaur* flew the flag of Vice-Admiral R. F. Elkins CB DSO, but this exercise too was marred by a fatality when, during the afternoon of Tuesday 3 April, a member of the flight deck personnel was killed in a flight deck accident. That evening he was buried at sea off Singapore and next morning the *Centaur* made a ceremonial entry into Singapore Naval Base, this time for a two-week visit. During this time, among other activities, a party was held for 300 children whose ages ranged from six to 14 years, and the First Sea Lord, Admiral Lord Mountbatten, who had been C-in-C Mediterranean Fleet when he had last visited *Centaur*, came on board and addressed the ship's company.

The passage home for the ships' companies of both *Centaur* and *Albion* was a far more relaxed affair than the outward voyage had been and there was almost an 'end of term' atmosphere on board the two carriers when they left Singapore on Saturday 21 April, bound for Suez. Five days later the Crossing the Line ceremony took place as *Centaur* steamed south of the equator for the first time during the commission. During the last weekend of April the ship's

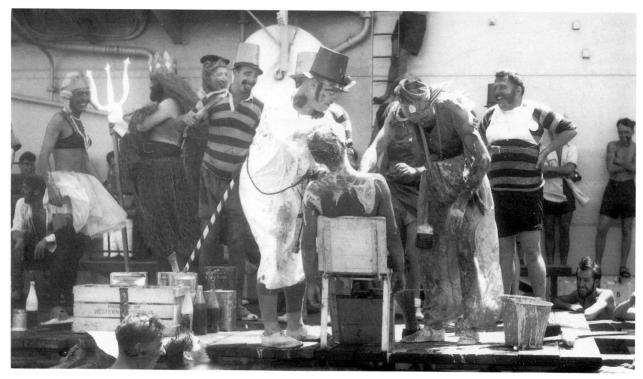

Thursday 26 April 1956, when *Centaur* 'Crossed the Line' for the first time. The victim is about to be ducked. *(R. F. Bennett)*

helicopter made a number of passenger trips for members of the ship's company. On Thursday 3 May the *Centaur* made her northbound transit of the Suez Canal and four days later she called briefly at Grand Harbour before continuing the homeward voyage. After a stop of only 48 hours at Gibraltar, the *Centaur* resumed her passage home and once all her squadrons had flown off she anchored in Plymouth Sound during the afternoon of Monday 14 May 1956, to await customs clearance.

It was the end of the *Centaur's* first commission, and she was now the first of the three sisters to undergo a long refit which, it had been decided, would be carried out at Devonport Dockyard. During the refit *Centaur's* hydraulic catapults would be replaced by the more modern steam catapults, an essential requirement for the launching of the much larger and faster naval aircraft such as the Scimitar and Sea Vixen which were coming into service. The *Centaur* was the only one of the three sister ships to be modified thus and it ensured that her career as a fixed-wing aircraft carrier would last longer than the *Albion's* and *Bulwark's*, both of which were destined to be converted to commando carriers.

After spending the night at anchor in Plymouth Sound, at 9.30am on Tuesday 15 May the *Centaur* weighed anchor and steamed up the harbour to secure alongside No 5 Wharf of Devonport Dockyard, where a large group of relatives and friends were waiting to greet her. On the weekend following her arrival she was opened to the public during Navy Days and later that month she was moved into No 5 Basin where most of the refit work would be carried out. On Thursday 14 June Captain Rolfe left the ship at the end of her first commission, which had lasted for two years and eight months.

The *Centaur* in 1956, shortly before she went into Devonport Dockyard to undergo a long refit. *(Fleet Air Arm Museum)*

On 20 September 1958, following her long refit, the *Centaur* anchored in Torbay when she spent the weekend at the seaside resort of Torquay.
(Fleet Air Arm Museum)

Chapter Five

Second Commission – Up The Gulf And Down Under

The *Centaur* remained in dockyard hands for over two years and during the refit the Bofors gun mountings which had been fitted on the flight deck, forward and aft of the island superstructure, were removed, and at the after end of the island a large Type 963, blind-landing radome was installed. It was on 18 August 1958 that the carrier's new commanding officer, Captain Horace R. Law OBE DSC RN, took up his appointment. At this stage, despite the fact that Commissioning Day was less than three weeks away, the ship seemed to be a confusion of wires, loose gear and unpainted metal amid the ever-present and incessant noise of windy-hammers. However, thanks to the efforts of Devonport Dockyard and a valiant band of cleaning ladies, the vessel eventually assumed a far more shipshape appearance and by the time the Admiral Superintendent's end of refit inspection took place on 1 September the *Centaur* was looking more like her old self. Next day the main drafts joined from the three naval barracks at Chatham, Portsmouth and Devonport, and no sooner had

they settled in than there was a rehearsal for the Recommissioning Ceremony which was due to take place the following day.

At 8.40am on Wednesday 3 September 1958 hands were piped to Divisions and the ship's company were mustered in the hangar where the Commissioning Service was to be conducted by the Chaplain of the Fleet, assisted by the *Centaur's* own chaplain. The short but moving service was concluded by Captain Law who spoke to his ship's company for the first time and informed them in a short address that the ship would be sailing for her trials as soon as possible. In fact it was to be sooner than most had imagined, for three days later, at 9.45am on Saturday 6 September, the *Centaur* slipped her moorings and steamed down the Hamoaze then through Plymouth Sound to start eight days of trials, which were relieved by a weekend break at anchor in Plymouth Sound. The sea trials resumed on Monday 15 September, with another break at the weekend when the *Centaur* anchored in Torbay, a location which kept the liberty boats busy plying between the ship and

The *Centaur* at anchor in St Helens Roads, off the Isle of Wight, on 13 November 1958. (*Fleet Air Arm Museum*)

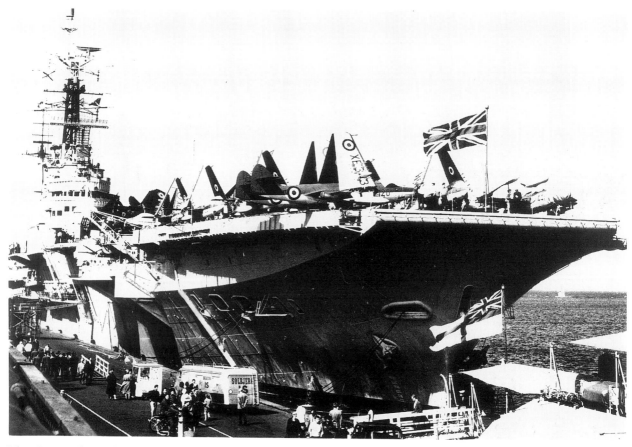

The *Centaur* alongside at Copenhagen in early May 1959. The frigate *Llandaff* is moored forward of her.

(Fleet Air Arm Museum)

Haldon Pier while the ship's company sampled the delights of the 'English Riviera' at the end of the summer season. All too soon, with the weekend over, the *Centaur* weighed anchor and steamed back to Devonport where she was to spend six weeks alongside 5 & 6 wharves, primarily to carry out deadload trials on the new steam catapults, and to make good the defects which had come to light during the trials.

On 23 September the C-in-C Plymouth, Admiral Sir Richard Onslow KCB DSO, visited the ship for just over three hours, during which he cast his eye over all he was shown and, to the irritation of the Heads of Department, also scrutinized a few things which were not on the schedule. During October, whilst the ship once again swarmed with dockyard 'maties' and organized chaos reigned on board, over 300 members of the ship's company took part in 'exped' activities which ranged over the southern counties and which were enjoyed by all the participants. On 6 November the Joint Experimental Helicopter Unit (JEHU), which was a joint Army/RAF unit flying six Whirlwind helicopters, joined for a week's

carrier familiarization, and on the next day, after embarking Admiral Sir Peter Reid KCB CVO, the Third Sea Lord, the *Centaur* sailed for further sea trials in the Channel. The trials team were embarked at Portland and then the ship left Weymouth Bay, after which 'Flying Stations' was piped for the first fixed-wing landings of the commission in the form of three Army Austers, which needed neither arrester wires, nor catapults when they took off again. The six Whirlwind helicopters flew the ship's Royal Marines detachment ashore on a mock assault exercise, and heeling trials made life awkward for everyone. Flying trials began in earnest on Monday 17 November with the arrival of the Sea Hawks of 801 Squadron, the Sea Venoms of 891 Squadron and two AEW Gannets from the Boscombe Down Trials Unit. For the remainder of the month flying was virtually continuous, with a short break on Friday 21 November when the *Centaur* spent the weekend in Portsmouth. After a further week of flying trials in the Channel, the *Centaur* returned to Devonport on 1 December so that leave could be taken by the ship's company. On the day after her arrival a Christmas dance

The *Centaur* steams up the River Tagus to Lisbon on Thursday 28 May 1959.   *(Fleet Air Arm Museum)*

The *Centaur* in the Mediterranean during June 1959. The Sea Venom 442 which is parked forward on the starboard side was lost off Tobruk on 25 June that year.   *(Fleet Air Arm Museum)*

was held in the hangar, with the most important guest being the television personality Marilyn Davies, who had been voted 'Miss *Centaur*'. During the two main leave periods the ship was stored and maintenance tasks were carried out, and it was Wednesday 7 January 1959 when she left Devonport to carry out further flying trials, being joined this time by a Sea Vixen and a Scimitar. It soon became clear that, despite a crash on deck when the Sea Vixen's undercarriage collapsed, the *Centaur* would be quite capable of operating these two new aircraft, although it would be some time before she operated them as part of her air group. The trials of the new aircraft proved successful, in spite of the weather, and later that month the Sea Hawks, Sea Venoms and Skyraiders of 801 and 891 Squadrons and 849D Flight respectively, were safely embarked, together with Whirlwind helicopters of 845 Squadron before course was set for Gibraltar. By Monday 26 January warmer weather was being enjoyed and Gibraltar Bay was a very welcome sight that morning when the *Centaur* anchored off the colony. Although she stayed for only 12 hours, leave was granted and for many it was their first encounter with a local 'brew'. However, despite a

few hangovers, the ship sailed on time to carry out her operational work-up off Malta. During this period one of 845 Squadron's helicopters ditched some five miles off the *Centaur's* port beam. Fortunately, the submarine *Tallyho* was very close to the scene of the accident and she was able to rescue the machine's aircrew and return them to the carrier. During the work-up some very difficult manoeuvres were successfully accomplished, including an RAS with the RFA *Wave Prince* at night in a force 8 gale, with wind speeds of between 30 and 40 knots. Finally, all the hard work was rewarded on Friday 6 February when, at 4.30pm, the *Centaur* made a ceremonial entry into Messina Harbour for a four-day break which was enlivened by a carnival in the town. As well as the fleshpots of Messina itself, a number of parties tried to 'conquer' Mount Etna, while others visited the nearby seaside resorts to sample different varieties of the local wine.

Following the visit to Messina work started in earnest once more as the second phase of the work-up got under way. This involved the *Centaur* in joint exercises with ships of the Mediterranean Fleet, and included night-flying operations over a period of ten days after which, on Friday

Alongside Gibraltar's South Mole on 7 June 1959 on her way east.   *(Fleet Air Arm Museum)*

20 February, the *Centaur* entered Grand Harbour for the first time during the commission. The carrier berthed alongside the Parlatorio Wharf during the visit in order to undergo a self-maintenance period. The *Centaur's* stay coincided with the British Government's decision to allow a relatively minor Welsh ship repair firm, C. H. Bailey, to take over the Naval Dockyard facilities, a move which the Maltese Prime Minister and the majority of the dockyard workforce strongly opposed. Nevertheless, Britain went ahead and set the takeover date as 30 March 1959, and in February the Admiralty issued notices to 6,000 dockyard employees making them redundant, but offering them employment with the new firm. This led to unrest and demonstrations which, very briefly, erupted into violence with stones being thrown and windows broken. At one stage, on Friday 27 February, two platoons of riot squads were landed from the *Centaur* to assist the civil police but, fortunately, they were not required. The whole affair had been clumsily handled by the British Government which, if it had listened more to the local people, could have handled the situation better and avoided the trouble.

The third phase of the *Centaur's* work-up began on 3 March when she left Grand Harbour, accompanied by HMS *Llandaff*. Flying started that afternoon and soon after the first launches a Sea Hawk crashed into the sea but, fortunately, the pilot was picked up by the *Centaur's* seaboat. However, nine days later, at 12.52pm, another Sea Hawk of 801 Squadron crashed into the sea on the carrier's starboard side, and despite the fact that the seaboat was on the scene within minutes, the pilot, Lieutenant C. A. Madell RN, did not survive the accident. That same night the ship encountered severe weather which caused some damage to the starboard catwalks, and during the early hours of the morning the *Centaur* stood by the Spanish vessel *Las Chercia*, which was in danger of being driven ashore on the North African coast. Later that morning the storm abated which enabled the funeral service to be held for Lieutenant Madell. The exercises ended with a mock 40-hour war during which there was little sleep for anyone, and it was a great relief when the ship put into Gibraltar for a 48-hour weekend break. The gale damage was repaired before she put to sea again, this time bound for Plymouth.

During the passage home the *Centaur* took part in 'Exercise Dawn Breeze IV', with both the *Eagle* and the newly modernized *Victorious*. As part of 'Blue Force' it was the Fleet Air Arm's task to fly off air strikes against airfields on the south coast of England, with the 'Orange Force', in the form of the RAF, doing their best to intercept the strikes and attack the three carriers with their V-bombers. To everyone's relief the *Centaur* finally arrived back at Devonport on Wednesday 25 March and leave could be taken.

Whilst the *Centaur* was alongside, the fire-fighting teams from her duty watch were rushed to the *Ark Royal*, which was berthed nearby, to assist in bringing a fire under control. Fortunately, the dockyard and city fire brigades were also quickly on the scene and the blaze was extinguished within two hours. During this stay in port the Whirlwind helicopters of 845 Squadron, having suffered technical problems, were replaced by Dragonflies for SAR duties.

By Wednesday 29 April 1959 the *Centaur* was ready to sail once again, but not before she had embarked 150 families of ship's company members who were able to watch the squadrons being re-embarked and other flying displays. After these special passengers disembarked in the afternoon, a party of cameramen came on board to shoot part of the film 'Sink The *Bismarck*', which included the flying of two old Swordfish aircraft (one of them flown by the test pilot Peter Twiss) from the carrier. If readers get the opportunity to watch this well-known film, the *Centaur* can be clearly recognized as the carrier which has a very brief role playing the parts of both the *Victorious* and the wartime *Ark Royal*. On the first day of May another 350 families were treated to a day on board the *Centaur*, and as soon as they had been disembarked that afternoon the ship left Spithead and steamed up the Channel and the North Sea to the east coast of Scotland for three days of flying operations off Lossiemouth. This was followed by a five-day visit to Copenhagen where the carrier berthed alongside Langeline Pier close to the city centre on 8 May. During the stay several parties enjoyed great hospitality on visits to the Tuborg and Carlsberg breweries, while others found the Tivoli Gardens a popular venue. Over 300 local children were entertained on board and, by all accounts, their consumption of iced buns exceeded that of the ship's company. Sadly the visit came to an end on the morning of Wednesday 13 May, when the *Centaur* set course for the Irish Sea and flying operations in company with the *Victorious*. On Sunday 17 May both carriers anchored in Tremadog Bay where they were able to join in deck hockey and volleyball matches and the *Centaur* received a visit from FOAC and the Parliamentary Secretary to the Admiralty. The exercises were followed by a four-day visit to Brest beginning on Friday 22 May, after which the *Centaur* proceeded to Lisbon, arriving on Thursday 28 May. The main purpose of the week-long visit was ceremonial and on the last day of the month there was a combined services parade, which included a contingent from the *Centaur*. After embarking a number of guests, including the Deputy Prime Minister of Portugal, the *Centaur* left Lisbon on the morning of Thursday 4 June and rendezvoused with the 1st Destroyer Squadron, *Solebay*, *Lagos* and *Hogue*, as well as the *Llandaff*, to give the VIPs an impressive flying display. That afternoon she steamed back up the seven miles of the River Tagus to disembark her guests abreast the famous landmark of Belem Tower.

Off Malta on 12 June 1959. A Gannet lands on whilst *Centaur* refuels from an RFA. *(Fleet Air Arm Museum)*

On her departure from Lisbon the *Centaur* set course for the Mediterranean, making a call at Gibraltar to disembark 849D Flight of Skyraiders, and replace them with Gannets of 810 Squadron, which entailed a massive changeover of stores and equipment. This was followed by 'Exercise Sandex' off Sardinia which involved an 'attack' by Italian underwater swimmers whilst the ship was at anchor, whose activities kept the *Centaur's* divers busy looking for limpet mines on the underwater hull.

The first real break in the busy routine came on 13 June when the carrier secured alongside Parlatorio Wharf in Grand Harbour for a week of self-maintenance. However, work started again in earnest when *Centaur* left Malta for the Libyan coast and 'Exercise Whitebait' with the US Navy's carrier *Intrepid*. During the exercises, at 4.15pm on Thursday 25 June, Sea Venom 442 was lost when it crashed on landing and ditched ahead of the ship. Fortunately, the aircrew were recovered safely by the seaboat and next day there was even time to anchor off Tobruk where many took advantage of 'banyan' leave. Two days later the *Centaur* anchored off Port Said to await the early morning

southbound convoy which she joined at 3.40am on Monday 29 June. A Suez Canal transit invariably engenders a holiday atmosphere (particularly when homeward bound) and this occasion was no exception, with the gulli-gulli man and his hapless collection of squeaking chicks, and the bumboatmen who make determined, and often successful, efforts to get one to part with money. This time, with the ship anchored in the Great Bitter Lake for an hour, there was even the opportunity for 'hands to bathe'. But once business was resumed, and on a ship with limited air-conditioning, the situation became more trying, so a form of tropical routine was employed with working hours from 5am to 1pm, which admittedly didn't really help the watchkeepers much. Nevertheless, the *Centaur* was now the principal strike carrier east of Suez and the main task of the commission had begun.

On 2 July the squadrons were flown off to RAF Khormaksar in Aden and next morning the *Centaur* herself was moored off Steamer Point in Aden Harbour for a short maintenance period. Apart from the drab duty-free shops, Aden was never a popular port of call but a number of the

The *Centaur* at anchor in the beautiful natural harbour of Trincomalee. *(Fleet Air Arm Museum)*

The *Centaur* and her escort HMS *Lagos* refuel at sea shortly before arriving at Brisbane. *(Fleet Air Arm Museum)*

more adventurous individuals, including the Royal Marines detachment, joined the Aden Protectorate Levies for a few days. One morning the Levies brought two rather reluctant camels out to the ship where they offered deck rides to anyone who was interested, with Captain Law and Commander Pope being the first to try out this unusual form of transport.

The stay in Aden ended on 9 July when *Centaur* and the 1st Destroyer Squadron left for the Persian Gulf and what was to be a very arduous three weeks. The carrier's task was to find out to what extent an aircraft carrier could operate normally in the sweltering heat of high summer in the region. En route to the Gulf the squadrons made a number of sorties over Oman in a 'flag waving' capacity and the pilots were faced with not only the problem of the terrific heat, but also the fact that the completely featureless desert landscape made navigation difficult. On board the carrier the temperatures constantly hovered around 100°F which led to the flight deck being renamed 'frying deck'. On 16 July, after carrying out flying displays for Kuwaiti VIPs, the *Centaur* went alongside an oil tanker jetty at Mina al Ahmadi, 30 miles south of Kuwait city. Most members of the ship's company went no further than the Kuwait Oil Company's Hubara Club, but some ventured out to see the new city of Kuwait which was being built from oil revenues and which was to dominate the world news some 32 years later.

After leaving Mina, and after having removed all the sand which had accumulated on the ship during the seemingly continuous sandstorms, an exercise was undertaken in conjunction with the Trucial Oman Scouts, before a 48-hour visit was made to Bahrain where the heir apparent, Sheikh Isa bin Salman al Khalifa, and other VIPs were treated to a flying display. There were sighs of relief all round, however, when on the afternoon of Tuesday 28 July the *Centaur* left the Bahrain area for Karachi and the relatively cooler waters of the Arabian Sea.

The visit to the former capital of Pakistan was, for many of the younger members of *Centaur's* ship's company, their first contact with the Orient and it was quite a shock to them, with the squalor of the overcrowded city bringing home very forcibly the problems of what are now called Third World countries. On board an ailment known as 'Karachi Belly' kept the ship's heads in great demand, and after the visit ended on Tuesday 11 August it was said that it took weeks to clear the ship of flies. Next day one of the ship's helicopters was lost, but fortunately the crew were rescued by the seaboat from the *Lagos*. That evening Admiral Varyl Begg, The Flag Officer Second in Command Far East Station, was transferred from the *Lagos* and course was set for the naval base at Trincomalee in Ceylon (Sri Lanka). However, en route speed was reduced when the starboard plummer block overheated, which necessitated recovering aircraft with only one propeller shaft running. Fortunately, this was repaired during two days at anchor at Trincomalee and on Monday 24 August *Centaur* left for a series of exercises which included the Indian cruiser *Mysore* (ex-HMS *Nigeria*) and the Battle-class destroyer *Hogue*. During the evening of 25 August the *Mysore* and the *Hogue* were in collision and a number of the destroyer's personnel were seriously injured. The accident brought the exercise to a premature end and after the seven casualties had been transferred to the *Centaur*, the carrier left for Trincomalee where they were landed at the Naval Hospital. During the time the *Centaur* was at Trincomalee the Prime Minister, Mr S. W. Bandaranaike*, made a brief visit to the ship, and on the last day of August the carrier left Ceylon and set course for Singapore.

On Thursday 3 September the squadrons were flown off to RAF Seletar on the north coast of Singapore and next morning the *Centaur* secured alongside No 14 berth of Singapore Naval Base. There was a great deal of maintenance work to carry out and during the weekend following her arrival the ship's company moved into the comparative luxury of HMS *Terror*, the naval barracks at Singapore, for the rest of the month, while the *Centaur* herself was shifted into the base's King George VI dry dock. Throughout this maintenance period the ship's company made full use of the magnificent facilities offered by the naval base, and many visited Singapore city where the Tiger Balm Gardens and the Happy and New World amusement parks were much frequented.

All too soon the three weeks of luxury were over, and on the last day of September the *Centaur*, flying the flag of FOAC, Vice-Admiral C. Evans, put to sea again, re-embarked the squadrons and steamed up the east coast of Malaya to the exercise areas off the island of Pulau Tioman, and on into the South China Sea. During flying operations on the morning of Wednesday 7 October a Sea Venom of 891 Squadron crashed off the starboard catapult and, tragically, both members of the aircrew lost their lives. Three days later *Centaur* detached from the rest of the fleet and set course for Hong Kong, where she secured alongside the north arm of the Naval Dockyard later that day. The stay in the port was short but there was still plenty of opportunity to see the sights of Victoria Peak and Wanchai. The carrier's next task was to take part in joint exercises with the US Navy's Seventh Fleet off the Philippines, but with a typhoon raging in the South China Sea, the manoeuvres were carried out instead en route to Yokosuka in Japan. For three days the *Centaur* came under attack by Skyraiders from the USS *Lexington*, and on 16 October a helicopter from the US carrier was involved in the real-life

---

* Mr Bandaranaike was assassinated in September 1959, only weeks after his visit to the *Centaur*, and was succeeded by his wife as Prime Minister.

The *Centaur* high and dry in the King George VI dry dock at Singapore's Naval Base during September 1959.

(Fleet Air Arm Museum)

rescue of a Sea Hawk pilot from 801 Squadron when his machine crashed. He was later able to return to the *Centaur* by way of the destroyer *Caprice*, five hours after the accident.

The *Centaur* berthed alongside at Yokosuka on the morning of 21 October 1959, to a tremendous welcome from both the local residents and the US Navy. Yokosuka is situated 30 miles south of Tokyo and the naval base there was taken over from the Japanese by the US Navy at the end of the Second World War. The *Centaur's* ship's company found the 'PX' a great attraction, as well as Tokyo itself, and a group of three cyclists even rode from the ship to the summit of Mount Fuji and back. The Royal Marines detachment joined up with the US Marine Corps for an impressive sunset parade, and a tea dance was held in the hangar to which over 100 local girls came, many in their traditional kimonos. One morning during the visit work stopped completely as everyone crowded onto all available vantage points to watch a display of dancing on the jetty. However, on 31 October it was time to say goodbye to Japan as the *Centaur*, together with her escorts *Lagos*, *Cavalier* and the Australian destroyers *Tobruk* and *Anzac*,

left the country for a second visit to Hong Kong, for a period of maintenance, before heading south for Australia.

At 1pm on Friday 27 November the *Centaur* crossed the equator at Longitude 138°, - 08'E, just north of New Guinea, and two days later she anchored off the small Australian base at Manus where recreational leave was granted before *Centaur* set course for Hervey Bay, off Bundaberg, some 180 miles north of Brisbane, where an opportunity was taken to touch up the ship's paintwork. With everyone eager to get to Brisbane, a few members of the ship's company set off in three whalers to try to make the passage before the *Centaur*. In fact, their attempt almost succeeded, with the ship only overhauling them in Moreton Bay. The visit to Brisbane was to be the highlight of the commission, particularly since it coincided with Queensland's Centenary celebrations, and as the carrier approached the port, the ship's company formed up on the flight deck with a centenary greeting. During the morning of Tuesday 8 December the Gannets and Sea Hawks of 801 and 810 Squadrons (the Venoms of 891 Squadron being grounded with technical problems), made a fly-past over the city of Brisbane, and at 6pm that evening the *Centaur* secured alongside Hamilton Wharf. The hospitality of the residents was overwhelming, with the ship's company being snowed under with invitations to parties in the city. Once again a tea dance was held in the hangar which was a great success, and when the ship was opened to visitors over 2,600 people came to look round.

The memorable visit to Brisbane ended on the morning of Monday 14 December when the ship sailed for Sydney. During flying operations en route, a Sea Hawk which had suffered a hydraulic failure made a successful 'wheels-up' barrier landing. During the afternoon of Wednesday 16 December the *Centaur* secured alongside the fitting-out wharf at Sydney where, once again, the hospitality was tremendous, and with five days' leave being granted to both watches and invitations from private homes coming from as far as 400 miles away, many were able to travel well outside the city limits. For those who remained in Sydney there were the beaches and the ice-cold beer which, according to the Aussies, is the best in the world. The ship received a visit from the Australian Governor-General, Field Marshal Sir William Slim, and a children's party was held, the high spot of which was the arrival of Father Christmas by helicopter.

The visit to Sydney ended on Tuesday 29 December, when the *Centaur* left the port and steamed round the coast to Melbourne, docking at Princes Pier on New Year's Eve to an appropriate welcome from the local Caledonian Society. After Melbourne the *Centaur* called at Fremantle, and during the voyage across the Great Australian Bight, a Sea Hawk slid from the flight deck into the starboard-forward catwalk where it had to be lashed and secured until the sea was flat enough to recover it. During the four-day

Two excellent views of the *Centaur* leaving the North Arm of the Naval Dockyard in the former colony of Hong Kong on 13 October 1959.

(Fleet Air Arm Museum)

On the afternoon of Tuesday 8 December 1959 the *Centaur* steamed up the Brisbane River to Hamilton Wharf in the city, where she took part in Queensland's Centenary celebrations. *(Fleet Air Arm Museum)*

stopover in Fremantle 90 disabled children from a local hospital were entertained on board, and they proved to be very popular with everyone who met them. The *Centaur* left Fremantle on Monday 11 January 1960 and en route to Singapore she anchored for 48 hours off the Indonesian port of Sourabaya (Surabaya), where just a few people managed to get ashore with organized leave parties. However, it was reported that contacts with the Indonesian Navy proved to be most friendly.

The *Centaur* arrived back in Singapore Naval Base, after an absence of three and a half months, on Thursday 21 January and after saluting the flag of C-in-C Far East Station, she was manoeuvring to go alongside No 8 berth when her port bow struck the jetty and neatly dropped the port anchor onto the dockside. It was said that the *Centaur* was the only ship ever to knock down a lamp-post in Singapore Dockyard. Unlike the previous visit there was to be little relaxation this time as FO2 FES, Admiral Begg, was due to inspect the ship and Divisions during the two weeks spent alongside.

When the *Centaur* left Singapore on Thursday 4 February it was to carry out a series of displays and manoeuvres for visitors ranging from children at the British Service Schools on the island to members of the island's government, following which she set course, ten days later, up the Strait of Malacca for Trincomalee. Once in the Bay of Bengal she and other ships of the Far East Fleet took

part in 'Exercise Jet 60', part of which involved embarking officers and ratings of the Indian Navy who had to familiarize themselves with the workings of an aircraft carrier before they took delivery of the *Vikrant* in the following month. During the exercise a Sea Venom was lost, but, fortunately, the aircrew were rescued by the *Carysfort*. After leaving Trincomalee on Monday 29 February, the *Centaur* steamed to the south-western coast of India for a 48-hour visit to the Indian naval base of Cochin, before leaving for the RAF staging post of Gan where she was to deliver some urgently needed aircraft fuel, before steaming on to Mombasa where she arrived on Saturday 12 March to join the Middle East Station once again.

Even before *Centaur* had tied up to her moorings in Kilindini Harbour, the ship's Dragonfly SAR Flight, piloted by Lt S. J. Hamilton RN, was involved in a dramatic mercy flight to transfer an injured European resident from the hospital at Mombasa to Port Reitz Airport, where he was transferred to a Nairobi hospital. The patient, Ian Pritchard, who had led covert operations against Mau Mau terrorists in Kenya and who had been awarded the George Medal for his outstanding courage, had suffered serious spinal injuries in a water-skiing accident and could not be moved by road, and Captain Law had responded quickly to a radio appeal which had been received while the *Centaur* was still at sea.

With the famous Harbour Bridge forming a backdrop, the *Centaur* leaves Sydney on 29 December 1959, to arrive in Melbourne for the New Year.
(Fleet Air Arm Museum)

During the *Centaur's* ten-day stay in Mombasa there were safaris to Game Parks and visits to the East African Breweries, the makers of the famous 'Tusker' beer. There were also swimming parties to Silversands Leave Centre as well as open days on board both the *Centaur* and her faithful companion, the destroyer *Lagos*. Sadly on the morning of Friday 18 March the visit was marred by a fatal accident involving the crew of the ship's Dragonfly helicopter, including Lt S. J. Hamilton RN, the pilot who had been involved in the mercy dash only six days before. The helicopter had taken off at 10.50 that morning on a survey flight to identify possible helicopter landing grounds for a 500th anniversary celebration of Prince Henry the Navigator which was to have been held at the Portuguese Consul's house in the Tudor area when, half an hour later, it hit an 11,000-volt power line across Tudor Creek in Kilindini Harbour. One eyewitness described events thus: 'When we heard the helicopter flying towards the creek the family and I went out into the garden to watch it. We saw it flying towards us, at a low height, when suddenly there was a vivid flash and a loud explosion. The helicopter passed in front of us, falling towards the water in staggering swoops. It was so close I could see the broken glass in the front. Then it hit the water about 30 yards in front of the house and sank just about immediately. It was all over so very quickly I didn't quite believe it was happening.'

Meanwhile, back on board the *Centaur*, the seaboats,

with members of the ship's diving team, were scrambled and they reached the scene soon afterwards. Unfortunately, the helicopter had sunk in 42 feet of water and it was not until 3pm that afternoon that the bodies of Lt Hamilton and his two crew members, Lt G. W. Smith RN and Naval Airman A. J. Roach, were recovered. The funeral of the three men took place, with full Naval Honours, at the city's European Cemetery the next day and it was attended by the *Centaur's* senior officers and a large number of the ship's company. Soon after this it was learned that the *Albion* was to take over from the *Centaur* as the east of Suez carrier, and that the latter would make her way home, but not before she had taken part in joint exercises with the Army off the Kenyan coast.

The *Centaur* left Mombasa on the morning of Monday 21 March and almost immediately she was operating her aircraft continually, first as part of 'Exercise Cormorant' off Malindi and then with the Army off the coast of Oman. On both occasions the Royal Marines detachment were landed and, it was said, they enjoyed the experience of operating with the Army. At just after 10am on Tuesday 29 March there was an unrehearsed exercise, dubbed 'Exercise Appendix', after a signal was received from a Lebanese merchant ship, SS *Checkmariel*, requesting help for a seriously ill steward. The *Centaur* rendezvoused with the ship and collected the man who, once on board the *Centaur*, seemed to make a remarkable recovery before being landed at Bahrain. On 3 April the *Centaur* made another visit to Mina al Ahmadi which, despite the fact that it was marginally cooler than it had been during the last visit, was still extremely uncomfortable. However, by now everyone's thoughts were turning to home as the *Centaur's* stint east of Suez was drawing to a close. On Wednesday 6 April she embarked Rear-Admiral Smeeton, the FOAC, who hoisted his flag in the carrier, and the following day she put into Aden for 24 hours. After a few days in the Red Sea, which were spent operating her aircraft, the *Centaur* anchored in Suez Bay on the evening of Sunday 17 April and the following morning she started her northbound transit of the Suez Canal, after which she ceased to be the operational aircraft carrier east of Suez. During the passage through the canal the holiday atmosphere took over and Admiral Smeeton opened the 'Easter Fayre' on the flight deck, where all sorts of stalls and a variety of buskers packed the flying area, raising in all more than £450 for charities.

After leaving Port Said the carrier made a fast passage through the Mediterranean, and after a brief 12-hour stop in Gibraltar Bay on Saturday 23 April she left for Devonport. Two days later all the serviceable aircraft were launched, and during the afternoon of Tuesday 26 April 1960 she berthed alongside No 5 wharf in Devonport Dockyard. Since her recommissioning on 3 September 1958 she had steamed 80,916 nautical miles and had carried out 7,805 catapult launches of her aircraft.

Although she was home again, the commission was by no means over, and after everyone had taken some leave she put to sea again on Monday 30 May bound for Rosyth, where she secured alongside South Arm Jetty on 3 June. During the ten-day stay she was opened to visitors and she received a visit from the Russian Naval Attaché, but it was all overshadowed by an accident on Sunday 12 June involving one of the ship's whalers which was out on a banyan outing with three members of the engineering department manning it. That evening a call was received from the Leith pilot that the boat had capsized, and although a full-scale search was commenced by the SAR helicopters and seaboats, sadly the whaler's crew of L(M)E M. J. Bird and M(E)s R. Maxted and H. D. McKirdy had drowned.

The visit to Rosyth was followed by flying operations off the coast of Scotland and a visit to Stockholm, where over 5,000 people visited the ship. From the Swedish capital the *Centaur* steamed down the North Sea and Channel, and after a long weekend in Portsmouth she carried out five days of 'Shop Window' flying displays before embarking several hundred families at Spithead during the afternoon of Tuesday 26 July 1960 and steaming into Portsmouth Harbour to secure alongside Pitch House Jetty. On the following weekend she was opened to the public during Navy Days at Portsmouth Dockyard and she proved to be very popular with the public, with 26,360 people going on board.

After that it was the end of another successful commission.

The *Centaur* at anchor in Weymouth Bay.   *(Fleet Air Arm Museum)*

Chapter Six

Third Commission – Problems In The Middle East

During the *Centaur's* refit in Portsmouth Dockyard a number of improvements were made to the living accommodation, the main one being an increase in the number of air-conditioning units on board. The ship's new commanding officer, Captain J. A. C. Henley DSC RN, joined the ship on Thursday 18 August 1960. Just over two weeks later, at 2pm on Sunday 4 September, a serious fire broke out in the ship's company galley which took the Dockyard Fire Brigade almost an hour to extinguish. Considerable damage was caused to the compartment and this took three months to repair. In the meantime the watchkeepers on board weren't inconvenienced as they were able to use the wardroom galley, but the remainder of the new ship's company had to be bussed into the naval barracks three times a day for their meals. Soon after this the ship moved into D Lock dry dock

where, as always when a vessel is in dockyard hands, organized chaos and confusion reigned supreme. There was an improvement in conditions on board when, in early January 1961, the *Centaur* was moved out into the harbour and berthed alongside Middle Slip Jetty. By the end of February normal routine had been restored on board and on the last day of the month the Flag Officer Air (Home), Vice-Admiral Sir Deric Holland-Martin, inspected the ship.

At one stage it had not seemed that the ship would be ready by the spring, but Friday 3 March 1961 dawned as a bright and sunny day and at 12.45pm the ship's sponsor, Princess Marina, Duchess of Kent, arrived as the guest of honour for the recommissioning ceremony. The Duchess had always taken a keen interest in 'her' ship and with her close relationship with the Wrens she often visited Portsmouth. The ceremony itself started at 2.30pm and the

Manoeuvres in the Mediterranean. This view shows Sea Vixens and Gannets on deck. *(Fleet Air Arm Museum)*

service was conducted by the Chaplain of the Fleet, with Captain Henley reading his Commissioning Warrant and the Duchess of Kent addressing the ship's company and their families who were assembled in the hangar.

Six days later, at 3.45pm on Thursday 9 March 1961, the *Centaur* slipped her moorings and put to sea for her trials off Portland. With the ship soon being put through full-power trials any 'cobwebs' which had formed during her eight-month refit were soon blown away, and by 17 March she was back alongside Middle Slip Jetty where the engineers could correct any defects. The carrier's flying trials were delayed because of problems with the arrester gear mechanism, and the first few days of April saw Gannets and Hawks carrying out touch and go circuits. On Thursday 6 April flying began in earnest when Sea Vixens of 893 Squadron carried out the first deck landings and launches of the commission. Three days later they were joined by Scimitars of 807 Squadron and eight Whirlwinds of 824 Squadron. No sooner were they settled in than the *Centaur* turned south and headed for the sunnier and warmer climes of the Mediterranean, and more flying operations off Gibraltar. It was whilst she was alongside in Gibraltar that the *Hermes* was encountered for the first time and the *Centaur's* 1st XI football team beat them 9-0. For the remainder of April and for the first week in May the *Centaur* operated in the exercise areas off Gibraltar and Malta, with only short breaks when she tied up to moorings in Marsaxlokk Bay or in Grand Harbour. She took part in air defence exercises with the US Navy's Sixth Fleet, in company with HM Ships *Camperdown* and *Lincoln*, and when these were completed she went alongside in Messina for a three-day visit to the port. Although this was the first real 'foreign' trip of the commission, everyone on board was waiting in eager anticipation for a summer crossing of the North Atlantic and visits to Norfolk, Virginia, Boston and Quebec, in preparation for which she went alongside in Gibraltar in mid-June for a short maintenance period and general sprucing up of her paintwork. However, the trip to North America was not to be, for the politics of the Middle East were to disrupt the *Centaur's* schedule quite unexpectedly.

On 19 June 1961 Britain had ended its protectorate of the oil-rich sheikhdom of Kuwait in the Persian Gulf, but as part of the settlement with the small state it had been agreed that military aid would be forthcoming if necessary. For some years after the Second World War Britain's primary reason for maintaining a military presence in the Arabian Peninsula was the need to safeguard the main sources of her oil supplies, which lay in the Persian Gulf. They became particularly important after the Palestine settlement created antagonism towards Britain, notably in Egypt, Iraq and Saudi Arabia. Of the oil producing states with which Britain was trading, Kuwait was by far the most significant and it was to her treaty relationships with Kuwait that Britain attached the greatest importance. Although the history of Kuwait as an independent state goes back to the 16th century, Britain's interest started in 1899 when an exclusive agreement was signed by the two, making Kuwait a protectorate. The actual state of Kuwait occupies just 7,400 square miles of undulating desert in the north-west corner of the Persian Gulf, and it is bounded in the north and west by Iraq, in the south and south-west by Saudi Arabia and in the east by the Persian Gulf itself. Oil was discovered in the early 1930s and in 1934 a 75-year concession was granted to the Kuwait Oil Company, which was a joint Anglo-American undertaking. Large-scale oil production did not begin until after the Second World War and by the time Britain relinquished its protectorate in 1961 and handed over the reins of power to the Sabah dynasty (who have ruled over the country ever since), Kuwait was the sixth largest oil producing country in the world. Within the agreement of 19 June 1961 there were four conclusions which set the seal on Britain's relationship with Kuwait and these were:

1) The agreement of 23 January 1899 shall be terminated as being inconsistent with the sovereignty and independence of Kuwait.

2) The relations between the two countries shall continue to be governed by a spirit of close friendship.

3) When appropriate the two governments shall consult together on matters which concern them both.

4) Nothing in these conclusions shall affect the readiness of Her Majesty's Government to assist the Government of Kuwait if the latter request such assistance.

On 25 June 1961, six days after the agreement came into force, General Abdul Kassim, President of Iraq, declared that Kuwait belonged to Iraq on the grounds that, under the old Ottoman Empire, it was a province of Basrah - which was indisputably Iraqi territory. There is no doubt that this claim was provoked by the widely held Arab belief that Britain lacked both the means and the will to protect her interests and to guard her allies, but the British Government took Kassim's strongly worded statement seriously, as did the ruler of Kuwait who asked for Britain's military assistance.

Fortunately, during the years leading up to 1961, there had been a succession of contingency plans for a full-scale British military intervention in Kuwait, and as tension mounted in the Persian Gulf, the wheels were put into motion and forces were soon on their way to the area. HMS *Bulwark*, the *Centaur's* sister ship, was already in the Arabian Sea at the time and, as a commando carrier with 600 men of 42 Commando Royal Marines on board, she was soon on the scene off Kuwait. The *Victorious* was the operational strike carrier east of Suez and she had left Singapore for Hong Kong on Monday 26 June, but three days later, at 7.30am, flying was suspended and she altered course for the Persian Gulf. She arrived off Kuwait on 10

The detachment from *Centaur's* 824 Squadron who assisted with flood relief work during December 1961, at their base, 'HMS *Vulture*' in Kenya.

(D. Hooper)

July 1961, four days before Iraq's National Day, when General Kassim repeated his claim to Kuwait and started to move troops and armour south from Baghdad towards the Kuwait border. However, by that time there were over 6,000 British troops in Kuwait and the massive airlift was set to continue.

For the *Centaur*, which had left Gibraltar on the morning of Friday 30 June, hopes of the trip to the USA were fast disappearing, and after embarking stores at Marsaxlokk she made a southbound transit of the Suez Canal on Thursday 6 July, in company with the destroyers *Camperdown*, *Finisterre* and *Saintes*. Four days later she was moored in Aden Harbour, where she remained for 14 days at only two hours' notice for steam on the main engines while events to the north unfolded. By now even the most optimistic members of the ship's company had given up any hopes of ever getting to America and the break at Aden gave everyone an opportunity to sample the beer and beaches of the Mermaid and Tarshyne Clubs. As the days went by without any hostile moves from Iraq it became clear that Kassim had realized that his initial judgement of

Britain lacking either the forces or the will to back Kuwait was wrong on both counts, (as was the case again some 30 years later when his successor actually went further and invaded Kuwait). Nevertheless, the state of readiness continued and on 21 July the *Centaur* left Aden to steam north into the Persian Gulf to relieve the *Victorious* which then returned to the Far East. The *Centaur* took over the air defence of Kuwait on 1 August 1961 and she remained on patrol off the Mina Oilport until Tuesday 15 August, when she was released from the duty and ordered to return to Aden. Ten days after leaving the area off Kuwait the *Centaur* was making her northbound transit of the Suez Canal, homeward bound, and on the morning of Saturday 2 September she embarked families and friends in Plymouth Sound and steamed into Devonport Dockyard to start a six-week, dockyard assisted maintenance period. Not only were most of the ship's company disappointed by the cancellation of the trip to the USA, but another blow for the 'Pompey' men was the fact that the docking period was in Devonport and not Portsmouth. However, for 40 brides who were to have been married to members of the

Full-power trials east of Suez in January 1962.

ship's company earlier in the month and who had postponed their weddings as *Centaur* sweated it out in the Persian Gulf, it was a great relief to have the ship back in the UK again.

It was on Friday 20 October 1961 that the *Centaur* put to sea once again, and that same evening, in Lyme Bay, she recovered the Sea Vixens and Scimitars of 893 and 807 Squadrons respectively. After spending five days carrying out flying operations in some very rough autumnal weather in the Channel and Western Approaches, during which time the body of a missing yachtsman was recovered from a life-raft and taken to RNAS Brawdy, the *Centaur* set course once again for the Mediterranean en route for the Far East Station. After a brief visit to Toulon at the beginning of November, the remainder of the month was spent in the naval exercise areas off Malta, where FOAC was embarked to carry out the ship's Operational Readiness Inspection. On completion of the inspection, which obviously must have been passed satisfactorily, the *Centaur* sailed for Port Said and on the last day of November she anchored off the Egyptian port.

The *Centaur* cleared the Suez Canal at 6.15pm on Friday 1 December and an hour later she rendezvoused with the *Victorious* to take over officially as the operational aircraft carrier east of Suez. Soon after this FOAC and his staff transferred to the *Victorious* for the voyage home to the UK, and the *Centaur* set course for Mombasa. However, before the ship reached the port, a detachment from 824 Squadron, along with one of their Whirlwind helicopters, had to fly to Lamu Island to relieve a similar detachment which had been left behind by the *Victorious*. Lamu Island lies off the north coast of Kenya, about 180 miles north of Mombasa, and it is about eight miles long and four miles wide. On the sheltered north-east side of the island lies the ancient town and port of Lamu, which in 1961 had a population of about 9,000, of whom approximately ten were Europeans. There was only one mechanically propelled vehicle on the island, a farm tractor owned by the Administration, which was headed by a European District Commissioner. There were a number of motor boats which maintained a ferry service between Lamu and Mkowe on the mainland, but the road between Mkowe and Malindi was often closed for weeks at a time during the rainy season, which isolated Lamu Island still further. The remainder of Lamu District extended north to the Somali border, south to the Tana River, and a few hundred miles inland towards the centre of Kenya. This hinterland was sparsely populated and the majority of the 30,000 inhabitants lived in coastal villages and offshore islands. In September 1961 the area was struck by heavier than usual rains with eight and a half inches being recorded in 24 hours. The resulting floods were widespread and extremely serious in the Lamu District. Fortunately, there was little loss of life, but inland communications were disrupted, livestock was drowned or marooned and crops were ruined. The River Tana burst its banks and the road link between Lamu and Mombasa was cut for about six months.

Lamu and the other islands, which could receive supplies by sea, suffered little, but the inland population was badly affected. Cargoes of maize were shipped to Lamu and Kipini at the mouth of the Tana River by local vessels, but little could be done to transport the goods to where they were most needed in the flooded areas beyond the coast. Landing craft from HMS *Striker* attempted to transport maize upstream from Kipini, but they had great difficulty in negotiating the swollen river which was still flowing at a considerably faster rate than usual. In late November 1961 two Whirlwinds from HMS *Victorious* arrived at Lamu, having been flown ashore as the carrier was passing Kenya on her way home to the UK. The naval party of three officers and seven ratings established a base on an area of open ground at the western end of the seafront. They christened it HMS *Vulture* and it consisted of a large marquee, a stack of 45-gallon petrol drums and a flag pole. Next day they set about the task of distributing tons of maize to the outlying villages and they left the task well under way when they departed for Mombasa on 8 December in the two Whirlwinds. Later the same day two helicopters from the *Centaur* returned with a new crew. Unfortunately, that night there was an unexpectedly high spring tide at 4am and the base camp was flooded, with water lapping over the helicopter wheels and some of the petrol drums being washed away. However, the new team carried on with the same schedule as the previous crew and the helicopters worked very hard, making several trips a day, with the ground crews often working until well after dark by the light of kerosene pressure lamps. The helicopters also made reconnaissance flights and casualty evacuations from the cut-off areas, and occasionally they provided the transport for police officers on enquiries. In fact, the personnel were real 'jacks of all trades' and their good work continued until 23 December when they left to rejoin the *Centaur* at Mombasa.

The *Centaur* spent Christmas at Mombasa and on Christmas Day the Deputy Prime Minister of Kenya, Mr Tom Mboya, visited the ship and stayed for just over an hour. Unfortunately, two days later, the celebrations were well and truly interrupted when General Kassim directed more threats against Kuwait and early on the morning of Wednesday 27 December the *Centaur* was ordered to put to sea and set course for the Persian Gulf. Initially it seemed that the *Centaur* might spend New Year at sea on her way to the Gulf but, fortunately, the crisis went off the boil, and on Saturday 30 December all the serviceable aircraft were launched to RAF Khormaksar in Aden, and on the following morning the carrier herself tied up in the harbour off Steamer Point. Most members of the ship's company did not relish the thought of ushering in the New Year in Aden but, in fact, the first day of January 1962 was marked by an afternoon departure from Aden as the *Centaur* left the port bound for the more exotic Far East with the prospect of a much more pleasant visit to Hong Kong.

During the voyage east the *Centaur* was accompanied by the frigates *Eastbourne* and *Plymouth*, and on 14 January she rendezvoused with HMS *Alert*, flying the flag of the C-in-C Far East Station, and after firing a 17-gun salute, the *Centaur* continued her voyage beyond Singapore, into the South China Sea. During the afternoon of Tuesday 16 January she ran into severe storms which necessitated the weather decks being put out of bounds, but the following afternoon she secured alongside the North Arm of Hong Kong Dockyard. Unfortunately, the seven-day stay in Hong Kong passed all too quickly, and laden with camphorwood chests and other oriental curios the *Centaur* put to sea again, bound for Singapore. At 6pm on Saturday 27 January, just 31 hours after leaving harbour, she received an emergency call from the oil tanker *Stanvac Sumatra* which had run aground and broken in two some 400 miles north of the *Centaur's* position. Captain Henley immediately altered course towards the wrecked tanker, but it soon became clear that other ships were on hand and that the carrier's help would not be required. Two days later the *Centaur* arrived off Singapore where she carried out preparations for a combined fleet exercise, 'Jet 62'. During these operations she lost a Whirlwind helicopter, but fortunately the crew of three were recovered safely. On the first day of February 1962 the *Centaur* berthed in Singapore for an 18-day maintenance period, before she set sail for the beautiful harbour of Trincomalee and 'Exercise Jet 62'.

The *Centaur* arrived at Trincomalee on Monday 26 February 1962 and Rear-Admiral J. B. Frewen, the Flag Officer Second in Command Far East Station (FO2 FES), transferred his flag to the carrier from the cruiser *Belfast*. The exercise began on 2 March in company with other ships of the fleet, including the destroyer *Caprice*, the frigates *Rhyl* and *Plymouth*, the cruiser *Belfast* and the INS *Vikrant* (formerly HMS *Hercules*), which was flying the flag of the C-in-C of the Indian Navy. The exercise was a very busy time for all the ship's company and on the morning of Wednesday 7 March, 807 Squadron's Scimitar XD 319 crashed in the Bay of Bengal, but happily the pilot was rescued safely. The squadron usually consisted of six aircraft, and by early 1962 they were being used as interim strike aircraft until the Buccaneer squadrons were formed. As Scimitars were being phased out of service and replacement aircraft were not yet available, it had been decided to disband the squadron. During the exercise Captain Henley had some words of praise for the *Vikrant* which he described as a '...delight to work with. We were impressed with the efficiency of her flying operations, in particular with her cleanliness and spruce appearance.'

At the conclusion of 'Exercise Jet 62' the whole fleet assembled at Pulau Langkowi, and many of the *Centaur's* ship's company sampled the delights of a real tropical island. However, by 12 March it was time to head west once again to prepare a flying display for Aden Forces Week and on Friday 23 March *Centaur* berthed in Aden Harbour, where she was visited by the Minister of Defence. However, the highlight of the *Centaur's* stay was the arrival of HMS *Ark Royal* at Aden to 'take the weight' of being the operational aircraft carrier east of Suez. Four days later, at 11am on Saturday 31 March, the *Centaur* left Aden for the Mediterranean, making her northbound passage through the Suez Canal on 4 April. However, before she returned to the UK she rendezvoused with ships of the 5th Frigate Squadron, including the *Ursa* and the *Scarborough*, for a four-day visit to Istanbul. This was followed by a two-week maintenance period alongside Parlatorio Wharf in Grand Harbour, during which time the Pipe Band of the Royal Highland Fusiliers gave a stirring display on the flight deck.

The *Centaur* left Malta on Thursday 3 May, and before setting course for Gibraltar she took part in anti-submarine exercises with the *Scarborough* and the *Broadsword*, during which one of her Whirlwind helicopters crashed into the sea, but the crew were rescued and returned safely to the ship. The two-day stopover in Gibraltar was popular for the last-minute shopping runs, but there was relief when the *Centaur* left harbour to give a flying display before setting course for Portsmouth. On Monday 14 May the aircraft were flown off to their stations and at 7.30am next morning the carrier anchored at Spithead for a short visit by FOAC and a much longer inspection by officers of HM Customs & Excise. It was nearly 11pm that evening before the ship obtained customs clearance, and so it was at 10.45am on Wednesday 16 May that she weighed anchor and steamed into Portsmouth Harbour where she secured alongside Middle Slip Jetty and hundreds of waiting families streamed aboard. Later that afternoon as HMS *Agincourt* was entering harbour and manoeuvring to her berth at South Slip Jetty, she collided with the stern of the *Centaur*, but the destroyer took the brunt of the damage.

During the *Centaur's* stay in Portsmouth there was a small but poignant ceremony on the flight deck to mark the departure and disbanding of 807 Scimitar Squadron, and at 10am on Monday 18 June 1962 Captain Philip G. Sharp DSC RN embarked to assume command of the *Centaur*, and shortly afterwards, at 11.30am, Captain Henley left the ship by whaler. Captain Sharp had joined the RNVR and was commissioned as a sub-lieutenant in 1937. When war broke out in 1939 he served in destroyers

and he won a DSC for his gallantry as the gunnery officer of HMS *Sikh* in a night encounter off Cape Bon, on the North African coast, in 1941. Having been forewarned by 'Ultra' special intelligence, *Sikh* and three other destroyers intercepted two Italian light cruisers carrying deck loads of fuel to Tripoli. In a short but brutal action the destroyers sank both cruisers with gunfire and torpedoes, and damaged an accompanying torpedo boat, with the loss of more than 900 lives, including their Admiral. In September 1942 the *Sikh* took part in 'Operation Agreement', a seaborne raid on Tobruk, the object of which was to disrupt the Axis supply flow on the eve of the Battle of El Alamein. Night bombing by the RAF had been intended to subdue the defences but, in fact, it ensured that all the defending forces were awake and at their posts when the seaborne raid took place. Both *Sikh* and her sister ship *Zulu* were sunk and Philip Sharp became a prisoner of war. Fortunately, seven months later, he was repatriated through Turkey and like many of the best RNVR men he soon had his own ship. He commanded the destroyers *Broadway* and *Cattistock* in operations in the North Sea, the Channel and off the Normandy beaches, and he was Mentioned in Dispatches. In 1947 he accepted a regular commission in the Royal Navy and he was the Executive Officer of the cruiser *Gambia* when she carried out relief work for the victims of violent earthquakes and tidal waves which hit the Ionian Islands in August 1953. He later commanded the destroyer *Defender* and was Captain of the Fleet, Home Fleet, before being appointed to command HMS *Centaur*.

No sooner had Captain Sharp settled in to his new command than he had to put to sea and head up Channel and then north to the east coast of Scotland for 'Exercise Fairwind VII' off Lossiemouth. During the passage the C-in-C Home Fleet, Admiral Sir Wilfred Woods, embarked by helicopter and hoisted his flag in the *Centaur*, and the Sea Vixens of 893 Squadron were safely re-embarked. After leaving the wet and very windy Scottish weather conditions, the *Centaur* berthed alongside the Überseebrücke Jetty in Hamburg at 2.45pm on Saturday 30 June for a memorable four-day visit to the port. Although the weather had improved little, everyone enjoyed the visit and few could forget the Royal Marines Beating Retreat in the pouring rain, a performance which received a standing ovation from the people of Hamburg. The *Centaur* left the German port on the morning of Wednesday 4 July to return to Portsmouth where she was to prepare for a series of 'Shop Window' displays commencing on Friday 13 July. With the enlarged 893 Squadron of Sea Vixens, 824 Squadron with its Whirlwind Mk 7s and 849A Flight, Gannets, the *Centaur* was the ideal ship to operate the displays and six separate programmes were carried out, with the Brave-class of fast patrol boats making mock attacks on the carrier. The displays were completed on Friday 20 July and after anchoring at

The *Centaur* steams up the River Mersey on a bitterly cold 31 January 1963, for a visit to Liverpool.   *(Mrs D. M. A. Sharp)*

Spithead that afternoon and the last guests had departed, the ship's company were able to relax during the weekend before *Centaur* was off once again, this time for a summer Mediterranean deployment, which included a docking period at Gibraltar.

On Friday 27 July Rear-Admiral F. H. E. Hopkins, the FOAC, embarked by helicopter to hoist his flag in the *Centaur*, and next day the carrier rendezvoused with the *Hermes* which was due to carry out her Operational Readiness Inspection. It was the *Centaur's* task to provide the opposition, before she berthed alongside the South Mole at Gibraltar where FOAC transferred his flag to the *Hermes*. On the last day of July the British India liner *Kenya* called at Gibraltar to disembark the Governor designate, General Sir Dudley Ward. That evening, as the new Governor drove to Government House, the *Centaur* provided a street lining party for this ceremonial occasion, while the Rook and Devil's Gap Batteries fired a 17-gun salute.

On the morning of Thursday 9 August both the *Centaur* and the *Hermes* sailed from Gibraltar to take part in 'Exercise Riptide III', during which the two carriers cross-operated with the US Navy's carriers *Enterprise* and *Forrestal*, and embarked and launched their Skyhawk and Skyraider aircraft. The exercise ended on the morning of Thursday 16 August when the fleet anchored off the Portuguese town of Estoril at the mouth of the River Tagus where the 'wash-up' was held. That afternoon holidaymakers at the resort were treated to the splendid sight of five British warships making a ceremonial entry to the seaside town of Cascais, just along the coast from Estoril. The *Centaur* led the column, with *Hermes, Berwick, Corunna* and *Crossbow* following in line. The two days off Portugal were followed by 'Exercise Alfex' in the Gulf of Lions, during which the two British aircraft carriers cross-operated with the French carrier *Clemenceau*, and both landed and launched the latter's Alize aircraft. This exercise was concluded on the evening of Monday 20 August, when *Hermes* detached to Majorca for a visit to Palma and the *Centaur* headed for Marseilles where she arrived alongside the next morning.

After an enjoyable four-day visit to the Cote d' Azur, the *Centaur* left for Gibraltar and her scheduled docking period. Shortly before she arrived alongside there was a rather novel silent launch of an engineless Scimitar, nicknamed 'Fred', which attracted a good crowd to see him launched from the starboard catapult and sink like a stone as soon as he hit the water. The *Centaur* arrived in

Gibraltar on the morning of Wednesday 29 August and that same afternoon she was moved into No 1 dry dock. The three-week refit was memorable for the hot, sunny weather interspersed with Levanters and on most days everyone could freshen up in both the mornings and afternoons when 'Hands to Bathe' was piped, and many took advantage of a 'dip' in the harbour. It was on 17 September that the squadron ground crews rejoined the ship and three days later the *Centaur* put to sea again, heading this time for the Aegean, with joint exercises with *Hermes* en route. Unfortunately, or, perhaps fortunately for most of the ship's company, gales disrupted the exercises, but the subsequent visit to Piraeus was a resounding success with the *Centaur* being berthed alongside a new passenger ship terminal in the centre of the city. In fact, she was the largest ship to use the terminal up till then and it proved to be an ideal berth for all types of runs ashore. From Piraeus the *Centaur* steamed to Malta where she embarked 11 squaddies for the voyage home. After launching her aircraft for Yeovilton and Culdrose on Wednesday 24 October, she arrived at Spithead two days later and by 1pm she was alongside Portsmouth's South Railway Jetty.

After only a two-week break at Portsmouth, which was extended for 24 hours because of a machinery defect, the *Centaur* left again on the morning of Friday 9 November 1962, and after re-embarking her aircraft off the Isle of Wight she set course for the Irish Sea. The immediate plans were for a series of exercises in the Atlantic as well as in home waters, and she left the Channel on Saturday 17 November to steam north for Greenock. However, throughout the whole weekend all flying had to be cancelled and speed reduced as the *Centaur* ploughed through severe storms with wind speeds of 48 to 51 knots and heavy seas. So severe were the conditions that the flight deck, weather decks and all sponsons were put out of bounds to non-duty personnel. Finally, by the early hours of Monday 19 November the *Centaur* was in the Irish Sea, about 20 miles south of the Isle of Man.

At 5.40 am that morning there was a sudden loss of pressure in A boiler room and a partial loss of electrical power as an invisible jet of superheated steam escaping at a temperature of 700°F, and with a pressure of 400 to 500 psi, burst from a main steam pipe in the compartment. However, on the bridge the only indication of anything being wrong was when steam pressure was lost on the port engine, which was fed by the boilers in A boiler room. The lights failed, radar sets tripped and initially thoughts were immediately turned to restoring power for the very safety of the ship. It was soon realized, however, that this was something more serious than a straightforward power failure when the watch in the engine rooms reported that they were unable to contact the four men on watch in the boiler room, or the engineer officer of the watch who was in the compartment as part of his rounds of machinery

spaces. He normally kept his watch in A engine room and he could only have been in the boiler room for a few minutes. Within a very short time emergency measures were taken to isolate oil and steam supplies to the stricken compartment, and to attempt an entry into the boiler room to rescue those inside.

The five personnel on duty in the compartment were Acting Engineer Sub-Lieutenant Leslie T. Jennings RN, Chief Engineering Mechanic Thomas H. Cartwright, Leading Engineering Mechanic Derick Hambridge, and Engineering Mechanics John E. McCosh and Gerald B. P. Fitzpatrick. All of them were killed instantly by the scalding jet of steam. Two members of the engineering department, Sub-Lieutenant John Shiffner and ERA Bernard Jolley, were quickly on the scene and they did not even stop to don asbestos suits before attempting to enter the airlock doors into the pressurized boiler room. When ERA Jolley tried to open the door the heat was so intense and there was so much steam that it was not even safe to open the inner door. He realized some awful accident had happened and he tried to get into the boiler room via a ladder in the downtakes but, once again, he was driven back by the terrific heat. He again tried the airlock but was unsuccessful and eventually, wearing an asbestos suit, he managed to get through the escape hatch where he saw two bodies. However, even when wearing asbestos protective clothing he could only stay in the boiler room for a matter of minutes and he was soon forced back out by the heat.

Meanwhile, within minutes of the accident, both engines had been stopped while engineers worked to isolate both A boiler and engine rooms, but at 6.20am it was decided to anchor the ship and 'half-ahead' was ordered on the starboard engine only. At 9.27am the *Centaur* anchored in Red Wharf Bay off Anglesey, by which time the rescue teams had managed to recover the bodies from the boiler room. The ship's Senior Medical Officer, Lt-Commander I. H. Colley, examined them and concluded that all five would have been unconscious within a minute, and dead within two minutes, caused in each case by exposure to extreme heat, with suffocation by steam being a contributory factor. An escape from the compartment, in ideal conditions, would take at least 65 seconds so it was clear that the five men stood no chance of getting out of the boiler room alive.

Unfortunately, the *Centaur's* troubles were not yet over and that afternoon, while Sea Vixen 465 was on the flight deck with its engine running, Leading Airman Campbell was sucked into the engine intakes. Fortunately, another rating who was nearby showed great presence of mind and managed to pull him out, after which he was flown by helicopter to RAF Valley with a broken arm. At 2.30pm that afternoon, as *Centaur* lay at anchor, colours were lowered to half mast in honour of the five men killed in A boiler room and 20 minutes later, with many of the ship's

Centaur is manoeuvred alongside Princes Landing Stage at Liverpool, overlooked by the Liver Building.

(Mrs D. M. A. Sharp)

company having assembled on the flight deck, the bodies, wrapped in Union Flags, were flown ashore by helicopter to RAF Valley and a memorial service was held on the quarterdeck. That evening, at just before midnight, all the main engines were ready to steam at 'half-ahead' with only B boiler room in operation, and the *Centaur* weighed anchor and set course for Portsmouth. Next morning, as the ship steamed off Lands End, the nine Vixens and three Gannets were flown off to RNAS Yeovilton. It was a greatly saddened *Centaur* that steamed back into Portsmouth at 9am on Wednesday 21 November, having experienced the worst moments of her career. The *Centaur* remained at Portsmouth until well into the New Year as the dockyard checked all the ship's main steam pipes. It transpired that the tragedy had been caused by a faulty flange which had not been sealed to the pipe where it joined the deckhead, and which had come adrift. All the indications pointed to the fact that the particular piece of pipework had been defective since the ship's construction.

On Saturday 19 January 1963 the ship played host to both BBC sound recording teams and cameramen for the recording of the 'Good Morning' radio programme and for 'Songs of Praise', which was seen on the nation's television sets two months later during March. Soon after this the personnel of 893 Squadron joined the ship and on the morning of Tuesday 22 January the *Centaur* put to sea again to embark her air group and to carry out flying operations in the Channel.

Six days later tragedy struck the *Centaur* again when, at 8.32pm on Monday 28 January, a Sea Vixen crewed by the Senior Pilot, Lt-Cdr D. F. Fieldhouse RN, and the Senior Observer, Lt S. N. Swift RN, of 893 Squadron, was lost during the course of a night recovery. Having failed to pick up any of the arrester wires, the aircraft's undercarriage collapsed before it crashed over the port side of the ship. Captain Sharp immediately stopped the ship and both seaboats were slipped to carry out a search. In the event the body of Lt-Cdr Fieldhouse was recovered by the planeguard frigate, HMS *Blackwood*, and it was returned to the *Centaur*, but the body of Lt Swift was not found. The search continued throughout the night and into the following day, but still with no success, and a memorial service for the two men was held on the *Centaur's* quarterdeck.

The *Centaur's* first visit of 1963 was to Liverpool and she arrived alongside the city's Princes Landing Stage on the afternoon of a bitterly cold day, with snow starting to fall as she was nudged alongside. Despite the atrocious weather, with heavy snow falling on the city during the *Centaur's* stay, the visit was a resounding success. It was still snowing when the *Centaur* left Liverpool and the weather was to have its effects on the ship's flying operations, as the Whirlwinds of 824 Squadron and visiting Wessex helicopters of 819 Squadron were required for urgent relief work in Wales and Northern Ireland.

On Wednesday 13 February the *Centaur* was in the Channel carrying out flying operations with the Vixens of 893 Squadron when, at 5.30pm, Captain Sharp's voice unexpectedly came over the ship's tannoy to announce news which he had received from the Admiralty that afternoon. In the Far East, President Sukarno of Indonesia who was known to have backed the Brunei revolt in December 1962, had made a speech declaring a policy of 'Confrontation' towards the proposed Federation of Malaysia, and he had started moving large numbers of troops to the border with Sarawak. In addition to this there had been further upheavals in Iraq where, on 8 February, Army rebels had seized power and executed the premier, Abdul Kassim, who had been the cause of so much trouble earlier in the *Centaur's* commission. With such uncertainties on the political scene in both the Middle East and Far East, the Government had decided to deploy two aircraft carriers east of Suez. The *Hermes* was already in eastern waters and the *Centaur*, it was revealed, was to be the second carrier. On 14 February the *Centaur* secured alongside Portsmouth Dockyard's Middle Slip Jetty, where both watches were able to snatch a few days leave and, in the bitterly cold weather, a massive quantity of stores was embarked while the dockyard worked overtime to renovate the arrester units.

Exactly seven days after arriving in Portsmouth, the *Centaur* left the port and, after embarking her aircraft, she made a fast passage to Port Said and on 1 March she steamed south through the Suez Canal. Four days later she was once again secured to buoys off Steamer Point and the barren rocks of Aden. For two weeks the ship's company were able to scour the rather dreary shops of The Crescent, and a whole range of visitors were entertained on board, from senior officers to British schoolchildren from RAF Khormaksar. After leaving Aden the *Centaur* carried out flying operations off the colony and on 30 March she set course for Mombasa, finding time for the Crossing the Line ceremony four days later.

Most of April was spent in Kilindini Harbour carrying out self-maintenance, and while this was not where most of the ship's company would choose to be, it was far better than being in Aden. However, in early May came the news that everyone had been longing for - *Centaur* could head for home - and course was set for Suez. With only a 48-hour stop at Gibraltar on the way, the *Centaur* arrived alongside North Corner Jetty, Portsmouth Dockyard, at 12.51pm on Wednesday 22 May 1963 where families and friends were waiting to welcome their loved ones. That afternoon a short paying-off ceremony was held in the hangar and two days later Captain O. H. M. St John Steiner RN joined the ship and took command, while Captain Sharp, newly promoted to Commodore, took command of the Royal Naval Barracks at Portsmouth.

Chapter Seven

Fourth Commission – The *Lakonia* Tragedy

In June 1963, as the *Centaur* started a five-month refit, there was some speculation in the press that she was to be converted to a commando carrier as her sisters *Albion* and *Bulwark* had been, but this rumour was soon squashed by the Admiralty who made it clear that she would continue to operate as a fixed-wing aircraft carrier. Her new commanding officer, Captain Steiner, had joined the Navy as a cadet in 1935 and during the Second World War he served in the destroyers *Ilex* and *Havelock*, and the cruisers *Frobisher* and *Superb*, and he was twice Mentioned in Dispatches. After the war he served in the cruiser *Ceylon*, then commanded the destroyer *Saintes* and was Captain (D) of the 3rd Destroyer Squadron.

On 27 September 1963, as the *Centaur* lay in D Lock dry dock undergoing her refit, there was a fatal accident on board when a 19-year-old dockyard apprentice was killed in a paraffin fire in an aviation fuel tank where he was working. During this final major refit the *Centaur* was equipped with a Type 965, long-range air search radar which was fitted on a lattice mast at the forward part of the

island. Captain Steiner had wanted the modern early warning radar, which was available, but the dockyard were unable to provide a suitable mast on which to mount the aerial. Captain Steiner hit upon the idea of removing the lattice mast from the destroyer HMS *Battleaxe*, which was laid up and awaiting disposal, and this solved the problem. However, this particular piece of ingenuity brought a formal rebuke from the Admiralty, but personal congratulations from Vice-Admiral Sir Frank Hopkins, the Fifth Sea Lord responsible for Naval Aviation. Although much of the carrier already benefited from air-conditioning, some mess decks still sweltered in tropical climates, and so ships which were laid up at Portsmouth were 'raided' and any small air-conditioning units found were removed and taken back to the *Centaur*. After she had left Portsmouth they were installed wherever they were needed most, and they certainly helped to make life more comfortable on board.

On Friday 18 October the *Centaur* was towed from D Lock to Middle Slip Jetty and no sooner had she been

The Dutch liner *Johan Van Oldenbarnevelt* in the Channel during the 1950s. She eventually became the Greek cruise ship *Lakonia*.

(FotoFlite)

On Saturday 16 November 1963, the *Centaur*, with her new radar mast and landing mirror, and with her ship's company looking very smart, leaves Portsmouth for her trials. (*G. Lees*)

An aerial view of the *Lakonia* in the Solent during her 1963 cruising season. *(FotoFlite)*

secured alongside than the submarine HMS *Porpoise*, which was leaving harbour, was caught by the ebb tide and carried towards the bows of the carrier, which she hit broadside on. The damage to the *Centaur* was very slight and her operational ability was not affected, but the submarine's sailing was cancelled and she had to return to her berth alongside the North West Wall.

Friday 15 November 1963 was Commissioning Day for HMS *Centaur* and the ceremony was attended by the C-in-C Portsmouth, Admiral Sir Wilfred Woods GBE KCB DSO. Mrs Steiner cut the magnificent commissioning cake and when Captain Steiner addressed the ship's company he stressed the fact that every man on board had his special part to play in the ship and that everyone must work as a team. He was certainly not going to be disappointed. Next day, at 11.45am, the *Centaur* slipped her moorings and put to sea for her post-refit trials. For 12 days the ship was put through her paces and she received a visit from Vice-Admiral Sir Frank Hopkins. By the end of November the *Centaur* was back alongside Middle Slip Jetty for some fine adjustments by the dockyard and for everyone to take some rather early Christmas leave before the carrier left for the Far East only a few days before the start of the festive season.

Meanwhile, as the *Centaur's* ship's company enjoyed

their last few days at home with their families, just a few miles away at 107 berth in Southampton's Western Docks, a rather elderly Greek cruise liner, the 19,000-ton *Lakonia*, was embarking passengers for the final and the most glamorous and sought-after cruise of the year. She was to make an 11-day voyage from Southampton to Madeira, Tenerife and Las Palmas, which was advertised as the 'Christmas Cruise' and '...a holiday you will remember and talk about for the rest of your life.' Her passengers were all determined to enjoy their Christmas of 1963 and they came from all walks of life, including a well-known actor, a baronet, the Master of Trinity Hall, Cambridge, a number of successful company directors and over 1,000 other passengers who had all spent a great deal of their hard-earned money on this special cruise which, for just a few days, would transport them from the cold, grey skies of Britain to the sunshine of the Atlantic Islands. The *Lakonia* had been cruising for only eight months, so what had she been doing before becoming a Greek cruise ship?

The *Lakonia* was launched on 3 August 1929 from a Dutch shipyard at Amsterdam, as the *Johan Van Oldenbarnevelt*, for the Stoomv Mij Nederland Line of Amsterdam, more commonly known as the Royal Dutch Mail Line, which ran a regular passenger service between

The burning hulk of the *Lakonia* on 24 December 1963, with the *Centaur* and another rescue ship standing off in the background.

(P. Yockney & G. Lees)

Republic of Indonesia and Ahmed Sukarno, who had been fighting the nationalist cause since 1927, became the country's first president. Following this it was clear that the passenger service between Amsterdam and Djakarta would be much reduced and in 1950 the *Johan Van Oldenbarnevelt* was transferred to an emigrant service between Amsterdam and Sydney, which kept her occupied for nine years until 1959 when she started a round-the-world passenger service, which was broken only by short cruises from Sydney. On one occasion she even served as a floating hotel for passengers from New Zealand who were attending the Empire Games being held at Fremantle.

However, by February 1963 she was almost 30 years old, which is a good age for any ship, and her owners withdrew her from service and put her up for sale. She was quickly bought by the General Steam Navigation Company Ltd of Greece who refitted her at Genoa for service as a cruise ship and renamed her *Lakonia*, after a district of the Peloponnesus peninsular. She made her first cruise from Southampton in April 1963, and the 11-day cruise which started on 19 December 1963 was to be the last holiday voyage of her first season.

On 18 December a surveyor from the Ministry of Transport at Southampton boarded the *Lakonia* and, according to regulations, he witnessed both fire and boat drills which were carried out satisfactorily. Boat drill required seven of the *Lakonia's* 22 lifeboats to be lowered to embarkation deck level, and four of these to be further lowered into the water, before all of them were returned to their davits.

Such was the background to the Greek liner when she left Southampton on the evening of Thursday 19 December 1963, on what had been a cold, dull and grey day, with 646 excited passengers, and a crew of 376. For all those who survived the tragic voyage it was to be a nightmare which they would remember for the rest of their lives.

The *Lakonia's* cruise director soon got the holiday atmosphere going with all sorts of fun and games, and next morning the statutory lifeboat drill was regarded by many of the passengers as rather an inconvenience on what was, after all, a holiday. By all accounts the session was not well organized, with no formal instructions to passengers on what to do in case of an emergency, or how to fit their life

Amsterdam and the capital city of the Dutch East Indies, Batavia (now the Indonesian capital Djakarta). She was named after a controversial Dutch statesman and she made her maiden voyage from Amsterdam to Batavia in May 1930. She continued on the route until just before the outbreak of the Second World War, when she made a voyage to New York as part of a charter trip for the Holland-America Line. Following the German invasion of Holland the *Johan Van Oldenbarnevelt* came to Britain where she was fitted out as a troop transport by Harland & Wolff, and for the remainder of the war she was based at Willemstad, the capital of the Netherlands Antilles on Curacao Island. During the war she carried thousands of British troops to all theatres of war and she continued to carry servicemen for a year after VJ Day. However, in late 1946 her charter as a troopship ended and she was returned to her owners who carried out a substantial refit, during which the troop dormitories were replaced once again with cabins, and her saloons and lounges were refurbished and restored to their former elegance. In 1947 she resumed her original passenger service between Amsterdam and Batavia, but it was not to last, for a vicious war was being fought in the Dutch East Indies between Sukarno's nationalists (who had actually been given independence by the occupying Japanese in 1945, which the Dutch had refused to recognize), and the Dutch Army. In December 1949 the Dutch East Indies gained their independence as the jackets correctly. For many it was a relief when the whole palaver was over and they could get back to enjoying the bingo, table tennis, horse racing, bridge and numerous other activities which were in full swing. As the *Lakonia* steamed south across the Bay of Biscay the weather started to get brighter and warmer and, despite the fact that there had been a large number of complaints about electrical faults, everyone seemed to be enjoying themselves. As the weather continued to improve and more passengers turned out onto the open decks, that evening brought the highlight of the day when Captain Mathios Zarbis hosted a cocktail party for all the passengers, where all the drinks were both plentiful and free.

By the afternoon of Saturday 21 December the *Lakonia* was steaming south off the coast of Portugal, while at just before 3pm, with her ship's company manning the flight deck, the *Centaur* was departing her berth and putting to sea, bound for Port Said and the Far East Station where she was to relieve HMS *Ark Royal* and join HMS *Victorious* as one of the two operational aircraft carriers east of Suez. There were tears in many eyes as, four days before Christmas, the *Centaur* steamed out of Portsmouth

Harbour and passed the Round Tower where many wives and sweethearts had gathered to wave goodbye. That afternoon she recovered the Sea Vixens of 892 Squadron and the two Gannets of 849B Flight and set course for the Mediterranean.

Back on board the *Lakonia* Sunday 22 December began with church services being held in the Atlantic Room, and the weather was now warm enough for the Lido outdoor swimming pool on the Sun Deck to be opened. All passengers had received a copy of the morning news-sheet, *The Daily Lakonian*, and many of the older passengers sat quietly in the public lounges completing the quiz and reading the programme of events. Other passengers bought tickets for the daily sweepstake which involved guessing the distance travelled over a period of 24 hours. For the more active there were the never-ending table tennis and deck tennis tournaments and the cruise director gave an informative talk, which he illustrated with colour slides, on the Atlantic island of Tenerife and Las Palmas, Gran Canaria. During the afternoon the Bob Hope film, 'Call Me Bwana', was showing in the cinema and a rehearsal of the Christmas Carol Concert was held in the Atlantic

The *Centaur's* helicopter hovers over the stricken cruise ship.

(P. Yockney & G. Lees)

Lounge. In the Lakonia Room there was more bingo, while elsewhere there was cha-cha dancing to be enjoyed. That evening, at both sittings for dinner in the Tropicana Dining Room in the forward half of the ship, and in the Main Dining Room aft, there were Christmas gifts for everyone courtesy of the Greek Line, and the main topic of conversation seemed to be the forthcoming arrival at Funchal on the island of Madeira, which was scheduled for 9am the following morning. After dinner there was all the gaiety and colour of the 'Tramps Tropical Ball' to which everyone had been invited and which was a casual evening with prizes for the best vagabonds, hobos and tramps. It was to include a tramps' sing-song and the selection of a Hobo King and Queen, and all the guests were to go dressed in their most informal and gaudiest outfits. By 10pm the ball was in full swing with the room crowded with 'tramps' and with the unmistakable sound of revelry as the band beat out the rhythms for the dancers, and with onlookers enjoying the party from outside on the Promenade Decks. About two hours before this, at 8pm, one of the ladies' hairdressers locked up the salon on the Upper Deck and went to her cabin for the night.

It was at about 10.30pm that night when the first passengers smelt smoke, and one passenger had noticed that the bulkhead of the hairdressing salon on the Upper Deck was almost too hot to touch. Meanwhile, in the Lakonia Room, Captain Zarbis was preparing to judge the best tramp and hobo costumes, when the first wisps of black, acrid smoke wafted across the room. Soon after this other passengers found smoke billowing around the passageways and staircases close to the Upper Deck and the alarm was raised. It was clear that the seat of the fire was in the hairdressing salon, and when the door was broken down it was also obvious that it had been burning for quite some time as the intense heat drove the firefighters back. Shortly afterwards the fire bells were sounded throughout the ship, but the lack of training in emergency procedures for both passengers and crew members was to have a deadly effect, for this time it was not just a routine fire drill but a genuine emergency with a fire raging and with passengers situated all over the ship in states ranging from merely sleepy to completely intoxicated.

The first emergency SOS signals were sent by the *Lakonia* at 11.30pm on the night of Sunday 22 December, and the first ship to reply was the British cargo vessel *Montcalm* which was on a voyage from Quebec to Casablanca. She soon altered course towards the Greek liner whose position was Lat 35° - 00'N/Long 15° - 15'W, which put her approximately 180 miles north of Madeira and 250 miles west of Casablanca. The *Lakonia's* first message had simply reported the fire, but it was followed 40 minutes later, at 12.10am on Monday 23 December, by a further report that the blaze was spreading. This was quickly followed 12 minutes later, at 12.22am, by the following message: 'Last time. I cannot stay any more in the W/T station. We are leaving the ship, please immediate assistance.'

As soon as the first message was received, the Norwegian salvage tug *Hercules*, which was based at Gibraltar, set sail, and at RAF North Front in the colony the RAF prepared to dispatch the first SAR Shackleton, to arrive over the scene of the stricken ship at first light. Very soon there were a number of ships heading for the *Lakonia* including the *Montcalm*, the Argentine vessel *Salta* and the Belgian liner *Charlesville*. The first one to arrive at the scene was the *Salta*, which reported at 2.35am that she could see the *Lakonia* on the horizon. At 3.29am the *Montcalm* reported that she had sighted a rocket and was almost in position. It was just over half an hour later that the *Montcalm* reported, 'The fire is blazing amidships but the hull not affected. Lifeboats sighted in the water.' It was clear that this was going to be a major disaster.

During the early hours of the morning both the *Montcalm* and the *Salta* searched the ocean for survivors and by 6am they had taken on board well over 200 people from various lifeboats. However, two signals from the *Montcalm* gave serious cause for concern, the first of which at 5.45am read: 'We have now taken about 12 people on board from *Lakonia*. Will continue searching area and also believe some people still remaining on fire-stricken ship.' The second, at 6.08am read: 'Boats 11 and 17 now alongside and people coming on board. *Lakonia* now exploding and fire spreading rapidly to all parts of ship. People still boarding and total figures as soon as possible.'

After the alarm had been raised on board the *Lakonia* the lack of proper training for both the crew and the passengers soon made itself felt. There was general confusion amongst the passengers who, without anyone to take command of the situation, just did what they thought best. Despite this lack of leadership some individual crew members did attempt heroic feats of rescue, in the main acting on their own initiative. One such example involved a Greek seaman who climbed down a rope ladder which had been hung over the ship's side in an effort to reach passengers trapped in their cabins. He did, in fact, manage to pull a ten-year-old boy, Nicholas Fishenden, through a porthole and get him to safety where he was reunited with his mother and both were able to get into a lifeboat. Sadly, that particular case did not have a happy ending. At least three boats capsized before reaching the water, and the occupants were flung into the sea. In one of these boats was Nicholas Fishenden.

The heat from the fire was so intense that four of the ship's lifeboats, which were situated above the Lakonia Room, could not be launched. However, by 2am all the boats which could be got away had gone, but there were still a large number of passengers on board, most of whom were gathered in the public rooms in the after section of

The gutted hulk of the *Lakonia* listing to port while the fire continues to rage. Her wheelhouse and bridge superstructure have collapsed. *(P. Yockney & G. Lees)*

A close-up view of the midships section of the *Lakonia*, showing the burnt and twisted metal of what had once been her lounges and bars.　*(P. Yockney & G. Lees)*

Steiner received a report from an RAF Shackleton that the *Lakonia* was still afloat and that her gutted shell was situated some 15 miles south-east of the main concentration of merchant ships. At 8.30am the smouldering hulk of the once proud passenger ship was sighted from the *Centaur's* bridge. By now the carrier's communications department had contacted and identified the 22 merchant ships, of 14 different nationalities, which were in the area. Captain Steiner then closed the biggest group of merchant vessels, who were recovering bodies from the sea, and ordered the *Centaur's* boats and helicopters away to check all the drifting lifeboats and life-rafts for survivors. It soon became clear that there were no survivors in any of them.

At 11.10am Captain Steiner decided to land one of his officers onto the deck of the *Lakonia*, and one of the senior engineer officers, Lt-Cdr J. Parry RN, volunteered for this duty. As he was lowered onto the smouldering hulk he reported that smoke was still belching from the after funnel, and from the ship's hull - from midships to the bow. The deck planking on the main deck had been burnt away, although the steel plating appeared to be intact. The *Lakonia's* quarterdeck, and the two decks immediately below it, had been burnt away except for a small section over which Lt-Cdr Parry was lowered. Amidships the superstructure had collapsed, but the shell plating of the hull appeared to be intact. There were jumping ladders, ropes and boats' falls hanging over the side and accommodation ladders had been lowered on both sides. Although the ship was trimmed evenly fore and aft there was a five degree list to starboard and on both sides of the ship there were two burnt-out lifeboats in the forward davits. As the helicopter hovered over the stern section of the ship, Lt-Cdr Parry sprayed the *Lakonia's* deck with a fire extinguisher in order to test the temperature of the deck and to ensure that he was not lowered onto scorching deck plates. As the foam from the extinguisher remained on the deck and did not dissolve in a sizzling hiss of steam, he considered it was safe to be lowered onto the blackened surface. The Whirlwind made several attempts to hover low over the deck, but even this manoeuvre proved to be difficult because of the deckhouses of the superstructure and the ensign staff at the stern. However, the helicopter managed to get into position and Lt-Cdr Parry was carefully lowered to

the ship. Also on board were several crew members and Captain Zarbis, but with all power lost there was nothing they could do to stop the spread of the fire, which by then was literally raging out of control.

A few hours later, at 12.15pm on 23 December, when the *Centaur* was some 50 miles south-west of Cape Finisterre, she was ordered to proceed '...At best speed to assist in the rescue of survivors of the liner *Lakonia* and to co-ordinate air activity through AHQ Gibraltar', including the USAF aircraft of the 57th Air Rescue Squadron from their base in the Azores. Captain Steiner immediately ordered full power and soon both the ship's engines were running flat out as the carrier steamed at 27 knots towards the stricken cruise ship. Whilst on passage to the scene of the disaster Captain Steiner ordered arrangements to be made to accommodate, feed and clothe large numbers of survivors and, on a more sombre note, to deal with the injured and the dead. Two Whirlwind helicopters and two Gannets were prepared for flying off at first light, and boarding, fire-fighting and towing arrangements were organized with all boats being made ready for lowering.

By 5am on Tuesday 24 December all the preparations were completed and at first light, when ships were detected ahead on the radar screens, two helicopters were flown off to carry out an initial search of the area and to locate the *Lakonia* as, during the night, one ship had reported that she had actually sunk. However, soon afterwards Captain

Lt-Cdr Arthur Coxon and his seaboat's crew approach the gutted hulk in an effort to board her. The starboard accommodation ladder and a number of rope ladders can be seen hanging over the ship's side.

(P. Yockney & G. Lees)

The *Lakonia* as seen from the *Centaur's* seaboat. The list of the liner can be clearly seen, and also the carrier's Whirlwind helicopter.

(Lt-Cdr A. Coxon)

the deck. When he actually landed he found himself on a narrow strip which had not been burnt away, and after cutting down the ensign staff he tried to explore the after section, but found that the edges of the deck tended to break away under his weight. As he looked down he saw that the innards of the ship were glowing red hot and he could feel the terrific heat radiating from the smouldering superstructure. He quickly came to the conclusion that there could be no one left alive on the ship, and after summoning the helicopter he was winched up and returned to the *Centaur* where he reported back to Captain Steiner.

From Lt-Cdr Parry's detailed account Captain Steiner was convinced that it was impossible for anyone to venture below to the *Lakonia's* lower decks, and that there could not be any survivors left aboard. It had also become apparent to him that all the bodies which had been floating in the immediate area of the disaster had been recovered. He then decided that it was important to carry out a thorough search of the whole area before darkness set in once again, because of the fact that not everyone had abandoned the ship at the same time and the gutted hulk had already drifted some 30 miles from the first reported position of the disaster.

By this time, because of fuel shortages, some of the merchant ships which had been standing by left the scene and Captain Steiner asked the remaining vessels to form up in line abreast to sweep at very slow speed towards the *Lakonia*, whose position he was able to hold on radar. He described the response as 'most commendable' and about ten ships of different sizes and nationalities formed up at distances of between half a mile and a mile apart, with the remainder following them. Once the ships had moved off, Captain Steiner ordered his helicopters to carry out a final search of the area, and then to concentrate on the area ahead of the formation as it approached the *Lakonia*. When they were about two miles north of the *Lakonia's* position he then asked the formation of merchant ships to reverse course and to do a second sweep in the opposite direction.

At just after 5pm the *Centaur* stopped close to the *Lakonia* and Captain Steiner sent a special boarding party, commanded by Lt-Cdr A. Coxon RN, to the stricken liner by motor cutter in order to try and establish more accurately the internal state of the ship. Lt-Cdr Coxon recalls that the liner was listing towards his boat and rolling in the Atlantic swell. He could see that the forward section of the *Lakonia* was still burning, and that fires were still raging down below. He noted that two lifeboat davits were still turned inwards, never having been used, but the lifeboats which once occupied the positions were completely burnt away. Just forward of the funnel, on the starboard side, there were two rope ladders which, he decided, were the only two which it would have been possible to climb. However, he noticed that not only were they very charred, but one of them was hanging by only

one side. In addition the ship's side was extremely hot, and so he decided that it would be far too dangerous to send anyone up them. Looking through the lower portholes he saw that the ship was almost completely gutted and that further collapse of the forward superstructure had occurred since the earlier boarding by Lt-Cdr Parry. Once Captain Steiner had received the report from the boat's crew he ordered the boarding attempt to be abandoned. The photographic staff from *Centaur* took photographs and cine film of the smouldering wreck as the ship's helicopters made a final visual inspection.

At 5.15pm that evening the tug *Hercules* closed the *Lakonia* and began preparations to take the liner in tow, and when darkness fell at just after 6.30pm Captain Steiner ordered the search to be abandoned. The last body had been recovered over three hours earlier, and the whole area had been very thoroughly swept. He was certain that there were no survivors either in the water or on board the *Lakonia*, and he felt that any further searching during the hours of darkness would be pointless, particularly as the last body had been extremely difficult to see in daylight and, even with a life jacket on, it only occasionally showed above the surface of the water.

All the masters of the merchant ships agreed with this decision and they were released from the search. Signals were sent out requesting any other vessels which were in the area to keep a good lookout. Some of the abandoned lifeboats had been towed away by the rescue ships, but it had not been possible to destroy the remainder before the *Centaur* left the area. These were reported by shipping for many weeks after the disaster, with lifeboat No 24 being sighted by the oil tanker *Texaco Hawaii* on 24 January 1964, some 80 miles from the scene of the disaster.

During the day the *Centaur's* boats and helicopters had recovered 30 bodies, and another 25 had been collected from the merchant ships which were at the scene, which gave the *Centaur's* ship's company the most gruesome job of all. A team consisting of medical officers, the dental officer, sickbay staff, Master-at-Arms and his staff, and sailmakers began the job of attempting to identify them, assessing the cause of death and canvassing them. Most of the bodies were those of elderly people, but for the staff carrying out this appalling task the most upsetting was the job of dealing with the body of the ten-year-old boy, Nicholas Fishenden, who was still dressed in his pyjamas and who had been rescued from his cabin porthole, but later lost his life when the boat he was in capsized while it was being lowered. It was also noted that he had suffered burns. On a different note Paul Yockney, who was a Leading Airman with the SAR Flight, recalls that the body of a Greek officer which he helped to bring back from one of the merchant ships had in his pockets over £2,000 sterling rolled into bundles, together with a lot of ladies' jewellery, and it was strongly suspected that all this had been looted from passengers' cabins before the man had abandoned ship.

All the bodies which had been recovered from the sea by the *Centaur* had been wearing life jackets and in one case an adult was even wearing a child's jacket. The surgeons noted that over 30 of the bodies had severe bruising around the chin, neck and face and it was thought that this had been caused by the impact of jumping into the water from the embarkation deck. They considered that the injuries were sufficient to cause concussion on hitting the water and, as the type of life jacket used would not keep a wearer's head out of the water, they probably drowned soon afterwards. This was consistent with reports from all the helicopter crews that the bodies were face down in the water. The medical officers also gave the opinion that the remainder would become unconscious after hours of exposure in the sea, and subsequently had drowned. Only three of the bodies had been mutilated by sharks, with typical teeth marks being noted on legs and upper arms.

By 8pm that night, as the *Centaur* steamed towards Gibraltar, 39 of the bodies had been identified but they had all been sewn into canvas and stored in the torpedo space aft of C hangar, packed with ice blocks. Meanwhile, the rescue ships were landing the survivors at Funchal in Madeira and at Casablanca. Altogether 128 people lost their lives in the tragedy, 98 passengers out of a total of 646, and 30 crew members from a total of 376. As for the *Lakonia*, she was being towed to Gibraltar by two salvage tugs when, at noon on Sunday 29 December, with the weather conditions worsening, her list increased suddenly and she sank about 250 miles south-west of Gibraltar.

The *Centaur* anchored in Gibraltar Bay at 4pm on Christmas Day and all the bodies were taken ashore by lighter. Captain Steiner was interviewed by BBC Radio News teams, and this was broadcast immediately before the Queen's traditional Christmas message. The *Centaur* sailed at 6.15pm that evening for Port Said.

The final word on the *Centaur's* vital role in this terrible incident should go to Captain Steiner who, in his report to the C-in-C Plymouth, paid tribute to his ship's company thus: 'Three satisfactory results emerged from this otherwise tragic and unpleasant operation. I could not have asked for better response or conduct from everyone in *Centaur*, many of whom worked without a break for very long hours. It would be invidious to single out individuals or departments as all were embued with the urgency of the situation. Undoubtedly however, those who had to handle the corpses had the most gruesome and trying tasks.'

The *Centaur* leaves Portsmouth for the Far East in December 1963.

(Lt-Cdr A. Coxon)

While steaming for home there is time for some relaxation on the flight deck.

(Lt-Cdr A. Coxon)

A very smart arrival at Aden on Sunday 5 January 1964.

(Fleet Air Arm Museum)

Chapter Eight

Fourth Commission – Mutiny In East Africa

After leaving Gibraltar on Christmas Day 1963, the *Centaur* set course for the eastern Mediterranean and after taking part in joint exercises off Malta with the *Ark Royal*, she arrived off Port Said during the afternoon of Monday 30 December 1963. In the early hours of New Year's Eve she entered the Suez Canal and by 7pm that day she was steaming south through the Red Sea. By Friday 3 January 1964 the *Centaur* was off Aden where, after a four-day stay in the port, her work-up started. During the work-up, on 15 January, the *Centaur* anchored off Aden and six Wessex helicopters and the remainder of 815 Squadron joined the ship from RAF Khormaksar, where they had been since disembarking from the *Ark Royal* on 19 December 1963. During the first two weeks of January they had assisted in 'Operation Nutcracker', which

Embarking 45 Commando, Royal Marines, at Aden for the fast passage to Dar es Salaam.   *(Lt-Cdr A. Coxon)*

was a demonstration of force in the Radfan area with a view to compelling the withdrawal of dissidents and convincing the tribesmen that the Government had both the intention and the ability to enter the area when it thought fit. However, no sooner had the *Centaur's* intensive flying operations restarted than world events intervened and, for almost ten days, the *Centaur* took on the role of a commando carrier.

Following Harold Macmillan's 'wind of change' speech to the South African Parliament in February 1960, the pace of decolonization quickened and it was accepted by the Government that in the course of a decade only a handful of British colonies would remain. Nowhere was this policy more apparent than on the continent of Africa where, just days after the speech, a new power-sharing constitution for Kenya was agreed which would give the Africans of that country experience of government prior to independence. On 9 December 1961 the neighbouring country of Tanganyika, which until the Great War of 1914-18 was German East Africa, was granted independence under Julius Nyerere, a socialist who wished to join his political ideas with the traditions of African village life. However, just off the coast of Tanganyika lay the island of Zanzibar which had undergone constitutional reform during the late 1950s and political parties had formed more or less along racial lines with the Zanzibar National Party being the dominant force under Arab leadership. The African majority had much less influence and shortly before Independence Day on 10 December 1963 the ZNP lost the vital support of the trade union movement. Soon after independence the Sultan of Zanzibar was overthrown by the underprivileged African majority, who also massacred their Arab co-nationals. These bloody events in Zanzibar were as worrying to President Nyerere as they were to the British Government who were the ex-colonial power, and he not only granted the deposed Sultan asylum in Tanganyika, but he also opened negotiations with the rebel government to try to effect a union between his country and Zanzibar. Two Royal Navy warships, the frigate *Rhyl* and the survey ship *Owen*, were sent to Zanzibar in order to help with the evacuation of British nationals. Initially it seemed that the disturbances in Zanzibar were internal racial disputes, but the unrest throughout the newly independent African states spread to Tanganyika itself, and also to Kenya and Uganda where it manifested itself in the form of mutinies in their respective armies. Following independence the

The *Centaur* steaming hard between Aden and Dar es Salaam. She has a very crowded flight deck with the aircraft, two RAF Belvedere helicopters and assorted military vehicles, all parked bumper to bumper.

(Rear-Admiral Steiner)

armies of both countries remained very much as they had been under the colonial governments, with the privates and NCOs being led by British officers. Measures were in hand to train capable local men for positions of command at all levels, but with the spirit of nationalism in the air there was no way that this process could proceed fast enough to satisfy the aspirations of some of the troops and on 20 January 1964 some men of the 1st Battalion Tanganyikan Rifles mutinied against their British officers at Colito Barracks just outside the city of Dar es Salaam. Ostensibly the mutiny was about pay and promotion in the Tanganyikan Army, but underlying feelings showed that there was resentment against the fact that British officers were still in command, and 30 of them were deported by air to Nairobi. For some time there was confusion in Dar es Salaam, with the whereabouts of President Nyerere a mystery and with the mutinous troops patrolling the streets and firing shots into the air. Fortunately, the mutiny was not followed by a massacre, but there was a certain amount of looting. President Nyerere was, in fact, safe and well and he immediately requested British military assistance to quell

the unrest. During the morning of Monday 20 January the C-in-C Middle East, Lt-General Sir Charles Harrington, and the Flag Officer Middle East, Rear-Admiral John Scotland, who were both based at Aden, had already ordered the *Centaur* into harbour in order to embark 600 men of 45 Commando, Royal Marines, in case they were needed to assist in putting down the disturbances in Zanzibar. By 1.15pm that afternoon the carrier was secured to buoys in Aden Harbour, off Steamer Point, and the embarkation of the men, their stores, equipment, vehicles, ammunition and two large Belvedere helicopters began.

Mr Denis Sparrow who was a Corporal Section Commander with Z Company, 45 Commando, recalls the events: 'We were based in Little Aden, which was a few miles up the coast from Aden town and right on the edge of the desert and a mountain range. We were carrying out training in movement and firing drills in the desert about ten miles away from the camp when suddenly, in a great cloud of dust, a Land Rover came screeching to a halt with an urgent message recalling us back to camp. We were driven back along the hot, dusty tracks in three-ton trucks which frequently got bogged down in patches of soft sand, when we had to get out and push, but once in camp there was the usual race to be first in the cold water showers. On this occasion we were told to pack our battle order, draw our weapons and prepare to move to Steamer Point to board the aircraft carrier *Centaur*.

Having loaded all our stores we drove round to the dockside where we were taken out to the *Centaur* in lighters and once on board we were given just enough space in the hangar for a camp bed, plus exactly one foot of empty space all round it with our weapons being stowed nearby. Having dumped our kit in the hangar we then had to load all our stores and ammunition which was very hot and hard work, but we managed to complete it by that same evening when we sailed from Aden, still unaware of our destination.'

Not only would *Centaur* carry her air group, but she would also transport all the men of a Marine Commando unit, together with 24 Land Rovers, 70 tons of stores and five Ferret armoured cars of the 16/5th Lancers. The commando personnel were accommodated on the quarterdeck and in the after section of the hangar, where the camp beds were so tightly packed that it was almost impossible to get from one end of the hangar to the other. Not only did the men have to sleep there, but they also took all their meals in the compartment. With the after hangar full of men, half of the ship's Sea Vixens were parked amidships on the flight deck, along with the stores and vehicles, and right aft the two Belvedere helicopters, which looked like overgrown dragonflies. At the forward end of the flight deck were three of the *Centaur's* own Wessex helicopters, while the small area still remaining was set aside for the Marines' exercise.

The Sea Vixens on the flight deck are almost hidden by armoured cars and Land Rovers.

(Lt-Cdr A. Coxon)

An even more crowded hangar with the 'sardines' of 45 Commando packed into their 'tin'.

(Rear-Admiral Steiner)

The 'sardines' come up for air.

(Peter Ames)

At 1am on Tuesday 21 January, less than 12 hours after she had arrived, the *Centaur*, accompanied by the destroyer *Cambrian*, slipped her moorings and left for the east coast of Africa. With all the additional personnel and equipment on board, a rather clever plan was devised to ensure that the *Centaur* could still operate her Sea Vixens. This was known as 'Sardine Stations', and it involved moving the Marines and their stores down the after lift, while the aircraft were ranged on deck by way of the forward lift. Shortly before any launch and recovery all the helicopters took off and hovered nearby until the operation was complete when, like a swarm of bees, they could return to the ship.

Denis Sparrow recalls life on board the carrier at this time: 'Once at sea we were told that the Tanganyikan Army had mutinied and that we would be required to land to assist in restoring order, and over the next few days we did intensive fitness and weapon training. Life on board was very cramped to say the least and we seemed to have to queue for everything, including meals and showers. However, the food was good and there was plenty of it.

What little time we were allowed on the flight deck was taken up with PT sessions, but in the evenings we watched films and played cards. As we passed Mombasa there was still no decision as to whether we would be required to quell the mutiny, but all the planning indicated that we would. With the Tanganyikan Army being British trained and equipped, nobody was taking its capabilities lightly.'

As the *Centaur* steamed south at 27 knots, Captain Steiner and the commanding officer of 45 Commando, Lt-Colonel T. M. P. Stevens MC, set about organizing procedures and drills for the various scenarios which they might encounter, but good land maps of the area were sadly lacking and so on the way south Captain Steiner sent a helicopter into Mombasa, where the aircrew were able to acquire Shell road maps, of the type which drivers usually bought at petrol stations. The carrier arrived in the Zanzibar Channel in the early evening of Friday 24 January and she lay out of sight of land while the *Cambrian* patrolled the stretch of water between Dar es Salaam and Zanzibar and made contact with the British High

A Marine of 45 Commando disarming a mutineer at Colito Barracks, Dar es Salaam and...

...armed landing parties from *Centaur* are taken ashore to secure the port area of the city.   (Lt-Cdr A. Coxon)

Commissions in both capitals, in order to report on the situation ashore to London, the C-in-C Middle East and to the *Centaur*.

At about 11pm that same evening a message was received from the British High Commission at Dar es Salaam requesting that the *Cambrian* close the capital and transfer VIPs to the *Centaur* as soon as possible. The message went on to specify the beach, the time and the light signals to be used, and to add to all the 'cloak and dagger' activity the *Centaur* received a message from a transmitter in the US Ambassador's residence at Dar es Salaam stating that, 'Countryman wishes to get closer to Westminster and will be at the ferry landing at midnight.' This was followed by a signal from London to the effect that the Royal Marines should be landed as soon as possible to disarm the Tanganyikan Army at Colito Barracks. Both the *Centaur* and the *Cambrian* moved quickly into the Msasani Bay area north of Dar es Salaam and, in answer to the first signal, the carrier's Executive Officer took one of the ship's motor boats, manned by an armed landing party, to the rendezvous where they collected Brigadier Sholto Douglas, the officer commanding the Tanganyikan Army. He was taken back to the *Centaur* where he arrived at just after 2am on Saturday 25 January to find that plans had been made for landings ashore. Brigadier Douglas reported that the 1st Battalion Tanganyikan Rifles had mutinied for the second time and had been rioting, looting and killing. He explained that the great majority of the mutineers were still living in Colito Barracks, which were a few miles north of Dar es Salaam, and that swift action was essential in order to keep casualties to a minimum. Another consideration was the fact that mutineers' families were living in quarters within the barracks and any heavy fighting was bound to kill or injure many innocent women and children. Captain Steiner, with the agreement of Brigadier Douglas and Lt-Colonel Stevens, decided to take Colito Barracks at first light with a plan that involved speed, an element of surprise and overwhelming force which would also involve a diversionary bombardment by the *Cambrian* firing 4.5-inch high explosive airburst shells over an uninhabited area just north of the barracks.

At 5.50am the *Centaur*, which had manoeuvred right into Msasani Bay, anchored in very shallow water, less than a mile from the shore and only three miles from Colito Barracks. Twenty minutes later, as dawn broke, the first assault wave of four Wessex helicopters containing Z Company, 45 Commando, Royal Marines, took

'Exercise FOTEX 64'. The *Centaur* off Pulau Tioman with HMS *Hampshire* and HMAS *Melbourne* in the background.   (*Lt-Cdr A. Coxon*)

'Exercise FOTEX 64'. RFA *Tidesurge* refuels *Centaur* and *Hampshire*. HMS *Dido* in the foreground.
(*Lt-Cdr A. Coxon*)

Hong Kong, March 1964. Another *Centaur* passes the carrier which is berthed alongside the North Arm of the dockyard.
(*Lt-Cdr A. Coxon*)

off from the *Centaur* for a landing site close to the barracks. At the same time Captain Steiner ordered the *Cambrian* to open fire with her diversionary airburst bombardment. For everyone involved this was the worst moment of all, since no one knew what was happening in the barracks, whether the whole of the 1st Battalion of the Tanganyikan Rifles was ready and waiting for them. As the helicopters reached the coast they flew well to the south of Colito and then turned north to run in upwind to their landing sites on the sports fields.

Denis Sparrow again takes up the story: 'We were woken in the middle of the night and ordered to get washed, have some breakfast, then draw our weapons and ammunition and prepare to move. I was part of Z Company and we had been chosen to make the initial attack, by helicopter, on Colito Barracks and my troop was to be the first to land. We moved from the hangar to the flight deck and as the *Centaur* turned into the wind our helicopter took off. At first we flew around the ship waiting for the RAF Belvederes to lift off, but they both had some sort of problem and we were given orders to carry on with the attack. HMS *Cambrian* was firing shells which seemed to be bursting above the barracks and our orders were that once we landed we were also to make as much noise as possible.

We actually landed on the barracks football pitch, which afforded us no ground cover at all and we felt somewhat exposed, particularly with the RAF's delay which meant that our ammunition was getting rather low. Some of our anti-tank grenades hadn't gone very far, nor had they exploded, and the incoming helicopters were landing right on top of the unexploded ordnance, but, fortunately, the rest of the company arrived without incident. With about 120 of us on the ground our company commander, Major Langley, took one troop for a left flanking attack on the main gates of the barracks and guardroom. First of all, through a loud hailer, he gave them a chance to surrender and when they refused, Marine Priest was given the order to fire a 3.5-inch rocket over the closed gates and into the guardroom. Unfortunately, it hit an overhead wire and rebounded, almost blowing up the company commander, but the second rocket hit the guardroom, blowing a pillar through the roof, killing and wounding a few of the mutineers and making quite a mess.

As the guardroom was cleared, my section was given the job of helping the company's Sick Berth Attendant tend the wounded men, one of whom had died after having had his arm almost blown off. Another, who had been hit in the chest also died, but one who had a nasty head wound we got safely back to the helicopter. I held his head as the SBA treated him, but I learned later that he died back on board ship. As we recovered the arms and ammunition in the barracks we covered the dead and marked them with upturned rifles which we stuck into the ground with their bayonets. We were then ordered to clear another part of the barracks and after doing this we moved to open scrubland beyond, where we were given cover by another troop. As we advanced, a machine-gun opened fire and, in fact, it came from one of our roadblocks which one of the European settlers had driven through in his car. He was very lucky to get out alive, but he was thoroughly shaken by the experience. Later we found a few more mutineers and took them back to the barracks. No sooner had we completed this task than we were off again, this time to the airport and then into the city itself. The next few days were spent patrolling the area and standing guard over a Tanganyikan Army parade ground while President Nyerere gave them a real dressing down, before disbanding them and sending them back to their homes. We were eventually relieved by 41 Commando, Royal Marines, and we were flown out to the *Victorious* with a feeling of anticlimax, but of having done a good job.'

The whole operation to quell the mutiny in Colito Barracks had taken less than two hours and all three companies of Royal Marines had been put ashore in 70 minutes, which was a remarkable performance of which *Centaur's* ship's company could be proud. Later that morning the *Centaur* weighed anchor and steamed round to Dar es Salaam Harbour, where she anchored two miles from the government hospital. There a tug and lighters were commandeered in order to land the Royal Marines detachment, together with four platoons of armed seamen and the Ferret armoured cars so that the port area could be secured. All the British forces were greeted enthusiastically by the people of Dar es Salaam who welcomed the restoration of law and order.

Next day the Wessex helicopters spent a great deal of time flying ashore the stores for 45 Commando, whilst one company of Royal Marines flew 340 miles in commandeered civil aircraft, escorted by Sea Vixens, to disarm the 2nd Battalion Tanganyikan Rifles at Tabora. They offered no resistance and at the same time British troops, at the request of Presidents Milton Obote and Jomo Kenyatta, helped to quell mutinies in the Ugandan and Kenyan Armies. To support the operation at Tabora in Tanganyika the *Centaur* reverted to her role as a strike carrier and launched her Sea Vixens to cover the assault with dummy ground attacks and low flying. Meanwhile, back at Dar es Salaam, Captain Steiner won over many local people by allowing the Royal Marines Band, in full tropical uniform complete with white helmets, to play in the main city square, to the obvious delight of thousands of spectators. A flying display was organized and a number of prominent citizens, including the Vice-President of Tanganyika, were entertained to a day at sea. Before leaving, Captain Steiner was invited ashore to a diplomatic reception, and at 7.30am on Wednesday 29 January HMS *Victorious* arrived to relieve the *Centaur*, which sailed for Mombasa just over eight hours later. Within 36 hours of

President Nyerere's call for assistance the mutinies within his army had been quelled and order had been restored. It had been accomplished with little loss of life in the attack on the guardroom at Colito Barracks, and the injured mutineers had been treated on board the *Centaur*. The Government might have ruled out her conversion to a commando carrier, but *Centaur's* ship's company had shown that for a limited period they could manage the joint roles of strike and commando carrier. As it happened, HMS *Albion* was east of Suez, but she was in Singapore at the time of the mutinies and her squadrons were fully committed in Borneo with the Indonesian Confrontation. She was nearing the end of a 17-month stint on the Far East Station and in February 1964 she was sent west to Mombasa, but by the time she arrived the unrest was over and she was only able to return 45 Commando and the two RAF Belvederes to Aden. I was serving in *Albion* at the time, and there was a great deal of uncertainty as to whether the East African unrest would delay the ship's return to Portsmouth. Fortunately, it didn't.

As the *Albion* steamed north, the *Centaur* left Mombasa with the *Cambrian* and set course for Singapore. This time the passage was far more leisurely and there was even time to celebrate 'Crossing the Line'. She arrived off Raffles Light south of Singapore Island at just after 7am on Wednesday 12 February, and four hours later she was alongside the Singapore Naval Base.

At last the *Centaur* was able to complete her work-up, this time in the South China Sea, and after two weeks of self-maintenance she put to sea to recover her aircraft. After four days the programme of flying exercises was interrupted for a 'Shop Window' display for members of the Singapore Government, including the Deputy Prime Minister, Dr Toh Chin Chye. The C-in-C Far East Station, Vice-Admiral Sir Desmond Dreyer, and the FOAC, Rear-Admiral Gibson, hosted the event, the purpose of which was to reassure the island's leaders that Britain would honour its commitment to defend Malaysia from its large and aggressive neighbour, Indonesia, which had declared its intention of destroying the Malaysian Federation. During the display the Sea Vixens screamed over the flight deck in a perfect formation and the SAR helicopters demonstrated a rescue at sea and an airlift of commandos. As a finale the Sea Vixens were joined by RAF Victor and Canberra bombers, Javelins and Hunters for a ceremonial fly-past. This public display was obviously also intended as a message to President Sukarno of Indonesia, who was not invited to the demonstration.

At the end of another week's hard work, during the afternoon of Friday 13 March, the *Centaur* secured alongside the US Naval Base at Subic Bay for a weekend of relaxation and, for many, an introduction to the never to be forgotten metropolis of Olongapo. This was followed by more hard work in the Subic Bay exercise areas where 892

Squadron carried out a weapon training programme in the form of bombing exercises. On the conclusion of the exercises ten days later the carrier set course for Hong Kong where, on the morning of Saturday 28 March, she secured alongside the dockyard's North Arm. During the stay in the colony the social programme took on more importance than exercise schedules. There was a visit from the Secretary of State for Defence, Lord Carrington, some first-class entertainment from local acrobats and jugglers, the bright lights of Wanchai and even a 'double take', when another *Centaur* in the form of the brand new 8,200-ton Blue Funnel liner, which was on charter to an Australian Chambers of Trade Mission, entered harbour. In every field of activity Hong Kong lived up to its reputation, whether it was shopping centres, restaurants, bars or even swimming at Repulse Bay, and it was with much regret that the visit came to an end on Monday 13 April and the *Centaur* set course for the exercise areas off the east coast of Malaya and her Operational Readiness Inspection, which was passed with flying colours and was followed by banyans on Pulau Tioman which, incidentally, more than 30 years later is a rather expensive holiday resort. The last two weeks of April were spent carrying out intensive flying operations in the same area, during which time a Sea Vixen of 892 Squadron made a successful emergency barrier landing with only one wheel. On the last day of April the *Centaur* was once again alongside No 8 berth of Singapore Naval Base. However, during the self-maintenance period, on Thursday 14 May 1964, a signal was received instructing the *Centaur* to sail for Aden to take 815 Squadron and their Wessex helicopters, who had embarked on the *Centaur* four months earlier, to the colony to continue support operations for 45 Commando, Royal Marines, in the Radfan mountains north of Aden colony, where a rebellion aimed at bringing down the South Arabian Federation had broken out. The six Wessex helicopters were detached to RAF Khormaksar on Friday 22 May, after the *Centaur* had made a fast passage across the Indian Ocean, and they went into action the same day. They were able to relieve the RAF Belvederes which were suffering serious mechanical problems due to the ingestion of sand into their engines. During the five weeks spent on these duties the squadron put in a lot of hard work and the helicopters were flown intensively with aircrews being airborne for up to six hours a day in extremely hot and uncomfortable conditions.

Meanwhile, after only 24 hours in Aden, which was quite long enough for everyone, the *Centaur* left for Mombasa and two weeks in Kilindini Harbour where she arrived on Saturday 30 May. Despite the fact that there was maintenance to be completed, there was also time for relaxation, which for some meant a journey to Tsavo Game Park or to Nairobi, while for others it was enjoying a pint of ice-cold Tusker beer at the Casablanca Bar. Many of the ship's company took the opportunity to travel up-country

The *Centaur* arrives at Hong Kong on 28 March 1964.

(Peter Ames)

by train to stay as guests of planters and afterwards the *Centaur* took over an Army mess in Nairobi wherè, after flying in the drinks from the ship, a suitable 'thank you' party was held. However, after leaving Mombasa on Friday 12 June, the *Centaur* returned to the area off Aden where the Sea Vixens assisted the RAF in making rocket attacks on the rebels in the Radfan area, in what were to be the final battles of the campaign. Although operations in the area continued, it was the end of organized resistance to government forces.

At the end of June the *Centaur* left Aden and set course for Madras, and en route she was able to assist the survey ship HMS *Dampier*, by taking on board a rating who was seriously ill with appendicitis. The visit to Madras lasted only four days from 2 July, which was probably a relief to most on board as, being a 'dry' city, the only group who appeared to have enjoyed the visit were the small but enthusiastic sailing team, who had two splendid days of racing. However, much to the concern of the Principal Medical Officer, many of the ship's company had brought parrots back on board and he wanted them to be destroyed. Captain Steiner disagreed and decided to give them a reprieve, and shortly after leaving the port the birds were perched on the tailplanes of the ship's aircraft, where they made a very colourful sight. Once the first aircraft engine was started up the birds flew off en masse back to their native India.

After leaving the eastern seaboard of India the *Centaur* steamed across the Bay of Bengal to the Strait of Malacca where, off the island of Penang, she took part in 'Exercise Buttercup'. On the third day of the exercise, at 8.27pm on Saturday 11 July, an emergency signal was received from one of 892 Squadron's Sea Vixens which had ditched in a position Lat 05° - 34'N/Long 99° - 34'E, but it was thought that the aircrew had ejected safely and all ships were dispatched to the area at maximum speed. The *Centaur* herself arrived in the area at just after midnight and she was soon investigating all sorts of reports of floating objects, which usually turned out to be logs or similar flotsam. At 4am a Gannet of 849B Flight was launched to assist the search, but just over four hours later the engine of this machine caught fire and it too had to ditch. Fortunately, the crew escaped unscathed and the search continued for the crew of the Sea Vixen, but without any success. During the evening of Monday 13 July an Indonesian destroyer was sighted by the *Berwick*, but it did not interfere and shortly afterwards, almost 48 hours after the loss of the Vixen, the search was called off. Next morning, at 7.50am, a memorial service for the aircrew, Lieutenant G. M. L. Terdre RN and Sub-Lieutenant M. J. Jackson RN, was held on the flight deck. Later that evening the *Centaur* anchored off Singapore and at 9.30am the next morning she made a ceremonial entry into the Naval Base where she secured alongside No 8 berth.

During the *Centaur's* stay there were outbreaks of communal violence in Singapore city, mainly between Malayan and Chinese youths, but the riots became serious at times and they were a great shock to an island which prided itself for its racial harmony. However, apart from leave restrictions to fit in with the curfew times which were imposed on the city, the rioting did not really affect the *Centaur's* ship's company, and on Friday 24 July she left to prepare for the major exercise of the deployment, 'FOTEX 64'. The programme of events got under way on Sunday 26 July with FO2's review of the fleet at Pulau Tioman, and this was followed by all the standard flying and anti-submarine exercises, with the thought of visits to Hong Kong and Japan to keep spirits high. Towards the end of the exercise there was a genuine case of 'Man Overboard', which is remembered by George Lees: 'A group of us were up on the flight deck sunbathing, when one of the chefs appeared and, without any warning apart from the shout of, "Tell her I love her", walked straight over the stern round-down and fell into the sea. Fortunately, we raised the alarm and the SAR helicopter was able to pick him up and return him safely on board.' George goes on to describe the conditions on board the carrier, which was not fully air-conditioned: 'Conditions on board whilst we were in tropical waters were pretty appalling, and my mess was made worse by the fact that we were situated aft and directly beneath the flight deck. Every aircraft that landed was well and truly felt by all of us and we often used to take our bedding onto the weather decks or gun sponsons to keep cool and get a good night's sleep away from the stifling heat of the mess deck. However, despite this I will always remember her as a happy ship.'

Following the completion of 'FOTEX' the *Centaur* returned to Singapore, but it was only for an extended weekend and on Tuesday 11 August she was at sea once more for 'Exercise Stopwatch' with the Australian carrier HMAS *Melbourne*, which was in commission again after her tragic collision with HMAS *Voyager* earlier in the year. The latter half of August saw the *Centaur* back in Singapore, but on 1 September she put to sea again, this time for operations in the Malacca Strait where she became directly involved in the Indonesian Confrontation. President Sukarno had decided to escalate the undeclared war by parachuting Indonesian troops into Malaya, near the town of Labis, and landing other groups on the west coast of Malaya. Although the incursions did not succeed and the intruders were quickly captured, there was a need for security forces to cover the west coast of Malaya, and the *Centaur*, with the helicopters of 815 Squadron and her SAR Flight, was well placed to patrol both the east and west coasts of the country. It was during these patrols that one of the Whirlwinds of the SAR Flight made a forced landing into a jungle clearing, but, fortunately, the crew were rescued safely. However, these patrols off Malaya

Homeward–bound through the Suez Canal, 13 December 1964. *(P. Yockney)*

caused the proposed visit to Japan to be cancelled. On 18 September, having left Singapore the previous day, one of the ship's helicopters made a forced landing in the sea, and despite the fact that rescuers were quickly on the scene, two officers of the crew were recovered unconscious and one rating suffered burns. The fourth crew member, Sub-Lieutenant Williams RN, was not found. Sadly the two officers died of their injuries and at 5pm that evening Lieutenant D. A. Dann RN and Lieutenant B. J. Gibson RN were buried at sea. Two days later, with a full war complement and a large escorting screen, the *Centaur* sailed for the hostile waters of the Sunda Strait to rendezvous with, and escort, the *Victorious* which was limping back into Singapore from Fremantle with her rudder out of action. *Centaur* was able to escort the '*Vic*' for the final leg of her voyage through the Java Sea and into friendly waters.

On Tuesday 22 September the *Centaur* left the east coast of Malaya in company with HMS *Hampshire*, and three days later she was once again alongside the North Arm Jetty of Hong Kong Dockyard for an enjoyable 17-day visit. However, with the weather scene dominated by cyclone warnings she was moved to No 1 buoy in the harbour, where it became a little more difficult to get to and from the ship. After leaving Hong Kong for the last time on Monday 12 October, she set course for Singapore with a short, 48-hour stay at Subic Bay en route, steaming within 90 miles of the eye of Typhoon 'Dot' which was raging in the South China Sea. The last day of October saw the *Centaur* alongside at Singapore Naval Base and on 2

November she left for yet more exercises in the South China Sea. On the next day, at 9.30am, flying was well under way when Whirlwind 'Bloop' of the ship's SAR Flight ditched alongside the carrier, and to add to the humiliation the second Whirlwind, 'Bloop-Bloop', refused to start, but eventually the crew of 'Bloop' were rescued safely by a Wessex of 815 Squadron. There then followed two weeks of patrolling the west coast of Malaya with the *Brighton* and *Falmouth*, and on 17 November *Centaur* went back alongside in Singapore. By now all thoughts were turned to 'home for Christmas' and on Wednesday 25 November the *Centaur* left Singapore to make a fast passage across the Indian Ocean, with only a short stop at Aden, to arrive in Suez Bay during the afternoon of Saturday 12 December, where she would await a northbound convoy through the Suez Canal. That evening the ship's company concert was held, and in the early hours of the next day she entered the Suez Canal for her 12-hour transit of the waterway. After leaving Port Said that evening she steamed hard through the Mediterranean and on the morning of Saturday 19 December all the serviceable aircraft were launched to their shore stations. The next day, at 9pm, the *Centaur* anchored at Spithead to await the arrival of HM Customs early the following morning. She finally secured alongside Pitch House Jetty in Portsmouth Dockyard at 2pm on Monday 21 December 1964, exactly one year after she had left the port. It had been a very eventful 12 months and ahead lay a short refit and, more importantly, Christmas and New Year leave.

The *Centaur* off Gibraltar.   *(P. Ames)*

Centaur and *Eagle* on joint exercises off Malta in May 1965.   *(Fleet Air Arm Museum)*

Chapter Nine

Fourth Commission – The Final Years

The first week of March 1965 saw the *Centaur* high and dry in D Lock dry dock, Portsmouth Dockyard, and while she lay there the announcement came on Tuesday 2 March that she was to be withdrawn from service in the following year. This made it clear that her next deployment was to be her last. The withdrawal would follow the completion of a two-year refit on HMS *Hermes*, and, in fact, *Centaur's* career had lasted longer than originally planned since the Conservative Government under Harold Macmillan had intended to withdraw her from service in 1963, but that was when the 54,000-ton CVA 01 was still on the cards for commissioning in the early 1970s. It was the confrontation with Indonesia and the decision to base two aircraft carriers east of Suez which had gained a reprieve for the *Centaur* and she had been manned with a ship's company largely taken from the

cruiser HMS *Blake* when that ship was put into reserve. In the event the *Centaur* was to be withdrawn far sooner than had been announced and she was destined to become the first of the Navy's five remaining fixed-wing carriers to go prematurely to the scrapyard.

In the second week of March 1965 the *Centaur* was moved out of dry dock back to Pitch House Jetty and 11 days later, during the afternoon of Friday 19 March, she slipped her moorings and put to sea in order to re-embark her squadrons and to carry out post-refit trials in the Channel. By the end of the month, with everything working satisfactorily, she was back alongside in Portsmouth, where she was visited by Lord Mountbatten and the last farewells were said before, at 5.45pm on Thursday 8 April, she left for Gibraltar and the Mediterranean. Four days later, after launching three

A pilot's eye view of the *Centaur's* angled flight deck.   *(Fleet Air Arm Museum)*

Vixens and one Gannet to RAF North Front, she anchored in Gibraltar Bay. The *Centaur's* arrival at Gibraltar coincided with General Franco's 'creeping blockade' of the colony which was designed to force the British Government to give the 'Rock' back to Spain. Customs restrictions at the frontier were intensified and action was taken to prevent Spanish workers crossing the border. Some Britons who lived in Spain and worked in Gibraltar had their permits withdrawn, and at the customs post in the border town of La Linea where 500 cars a day were once allowed through, this number was cut to ten. The generally belligerent attitude of General Franco, in the days long before both Britain and Spain were partners in the European Union, led to a great deal of uncertainty in the colony and the arrival of the *Centaur*, whose duties included providing the air defence of Gibraltar, gave a signal to the Spanish dictator of Britain's determination to hold the colony.

After carrying out her flying work-up off Gibraltar, the *Centaur* steamed to Malta where she continued intensive flying operations in the exercise areas off the island, and on Friday 23 April she secured to No 11 buoy in Grand Harbour's Bighi Bay. Next day the C-in-C Mediterranean, Admiral Sir John Hamilton KBE, and the Governor-General of Malta attended a reception on board. During the 12 days she was in Malta routine maintenance was carried out and the paintwork was spruced up for the carrier's first flag showing visit of the deployment.

On Wednesday 5 May, flying the flag of Admiral Sir John Hamilton, the *Centaur* left Malta and after recovering her aircraft she set course for Naples, where she arrived the following morning. After the four-day visit the *Centaur* returned to the area off Malta where, on Wednesday 12 May, she rendezvoused with the recently modernized HMS *Eagle*, which was returning to the UK from the Far East and had left Beirut two days earlier. Together they carried out two days of night flying exercises before putting into Malta on 15 May for four days before leaving again on Wednesday 19 May. However, this time the *Eagle* set course for Devonport and the *Centaur* for two more days of flying operations, during which time she encountered units of the Soviet Black Sea Fleet, including two heavy cruisers. She then set course for Istanbul, again flying the flag of the C-in-C Mediterranean, and after steaming through the Dardanelles and the Sea of Marmara she anchored in the Bosphorus at 9am on Monday 24 May. After four days in the ancient city the *Centaur* weighed anchor to negotiate the Dardanelles once again and steam down the Aegean coast to the city of Izmir, where she spent just under 24 hours before returning to the area off Malta once again.

During the first week of June the *Centaur* took part in fleet exercises in the Mediterranean with the cruiser *Tiger* and the frigates *Hardy*, *Russell*, *Penelope*, *Yarmouth* and *Falmouth*, and a day at anchor in Palmas Bay, Sardinia, provided the opportunity for many to enjoy banyan leave. By mid-June the *Centaur* was back in Gibraltar for a period of self-maintenance, and during this time the *Ark Royal* passed through on her way to the Far East. Other visitors to *Centaur*, and probably the most popular, were the Wrens from HMS *Rook*.

After leaving harbour during the early evening of Saturday 26 June, the *Centaur* remained in the Gibraltar area for the first two weeks of July, and during this period the Governor of the colony, General Sir Dudley Ward, who had been welcomed to his new office by the *Centaur's* ship's company exactly three years previously, embarked on board the carrier by helicopter for a flying display. After a further maintenance period at Gibraltar the *Centaur* left the Mediterranean for the last time on the morning of Monday 19 July and early the following day she steamed up the River Tagus to Lisbon for the last foreign visit of her career. The first three days of the visit were spent at anchor in the River Tagus, but for the last two she berthed alongside Alcantara Jetty, which was normally used by the cruise ships which called at the port.

The visit to Lisbon ended at just after midday on Sunday 25 July when *Centaur* set course for the UK, and she anchored in Plymouth Sound two days later, at 9.15am on Tuesday 27 July. At noon that day the *Centaur's* royal sponsor, Her Royal Highness The Duchess of Kent, flew on board by helicopter for a farewell visit to the ship which she had launched 18 years before and which had subsequently always been of great interest to her. After being welcomed on board by Captain Steiner, the Duchess made a tour of the ship and met representatives from all departments. At 1.45pm the *Centaur* weighed anchor and put to sea where the Sea Vixens of 892 Squadron and a Scimitar staged a flying display which lasted just over an hour before the Duchess of Kent bade a final farewell to 'her' ship and left by helicopter shortly after 3pm. That evening the *Centaur* anchored in Plymouth Sound where the 'ever popular' members of HM Customs & Excise boarded to levy their duties and to clear the vessel for the final leg of her operational career, a tour of British ports.

After leaving Plymouth Sound during the evening of Wednesday 28 July, the *Centaur* steamed down Channel and into the Irish Sea where, close to the scene of her terrible boiler room accident of December 1963, Buccaneer S2 aircraft, which had not then entered operational service, carried out touch and go circuits. On Friday 30 July the *Centaur* steamed up Belfast Lough to make a farewell visit to her birthplace, and at 1.30pm she was moored at the Aircraft Wharf, close to Sydenham and not far away from the slipway where she had been constructed. Although the bitter religious and political divisions were very evident to any visitor to Belfast, these were the days when British servicemen could still walk in the streets in full uniform

The FDO's nightmare. An RAF Vulcan bomber flies over the *Centaur*.　　　*(Rear-Admiral Steiner)*

The *Centaur* at Istanbul.　　　*(Fleet Air Arm Museum)*

The *Centaur* and the *Ark Royal* together at Gibraltar on 23 June 1965. The *Centaur* was due to visit Lisbon, while the *Ark Royal* was en route for the Far East. *(Fleet Air Arm Museum)*

and feel quite safe. On the last day of July the *Centaur* began a series of open days with a 'Meet the Navy' display in the hangar which proved to be very popular. Visitors continued to be welcomed aboard for the first four days of August, among them many groups of Belfast schoolchildren, and it was generally agreed that the event was a great success. At 6am on Thursday 5 August, at first light, the *Centaur* left Belfast and steamed out into Bangor Bay where she rendezvoused with the cruiser *Tiger*, the frigates *Berwick* and *Dido*, the fast patrol boat *Brave Borderer* and the minesweepers *Wolverton* and *Brereton*. After carrying out joint manoeuvres, all the ships made an overnight crossing to anchor next morning at the Tail of the Bank to prepare for a Royal Review of the Home Fleet.

The previous Royal Review on the Clyde had been in July 1947, when over 100 ships, including three battleships, had taken part. However, even in the immediate post-war years those leviathans, which had once symbolized the power of the Royal Navy, were already outdated and they had no practical role to play in the post-war fleet. By the mid-1960s the aircraft carrier had become the epitome of naval power and at the 1965 review the *Centaur* represented the new capital ship as well as being the largest vessel present. By Monday 9 August the fleet of 73 ships had anchored off Gourock, and among their number, as well as the *Centaur*, were the cruisers *Lion*, flying the flag of the C-in-C Home Fleet, and *Tiger*, the

depot ship *Maidstone*, the destroyer *Kent*, a number of frigates and a flotilla of minesweepers. The cruise steamer *Gay Queen* did a very brisk business providing shuttle trips round the fleet packed with eager sightseers from both Gourock and Greenock.

On the morning of Monday 9 August the Royal Family embarked in the Royal Yacht *Britannia* at Holyhead, after travelling from London by train, and set course for the Clyde. After stopping briefly in Kirkudbright Bay where the Queen and Prince Philip visited the nearby lifeboat station, the *Britannia* continued her voyage north. The morning of Tuesday 10 August dawned as a damp and misty day on the Clyde, but the ships were arrayed in three lines and dressed overall in true Spithead style when the *Britannia*, preceded by the flagship of the Northern Lighthouse Commissioners, *Pharos*, steamed past the Cloch Lighthouse, escorted by the frigate HMS *Aurora*, which was on station astern of the Royal Yacht. There was a glimmer of sunshine as the *Britannia*, with her brilliant blue and white paintwork, steamed by the lines of warships on the south side of the Clyde, and as she glided along 15 vessels of the flagship and frigate line fired a royal salute of 21 guns. Helicopters hovered overhead and bands played as the Royal Yacht dropped anchor. All along the esplanades of Greenock and Gourock the police struggled to cope with the cars which had been parked in every available space in the two towns by the thousands of sightseers who had

Full-power trial and plenty of black smoke.

A Sea Vixen is launched from the port catapult. *(P. Ames)*

Tuesday 20 July 1965 and the *Centaur* makes a very smart ceremonial entry into Lisbon on her last foreign visit. The Tagus Road Bridge is under construction.

(Rear-Admiral Steiner)

On Tuesday 27 July 1965, the *Centaur's* royal sponsor, HRH Princess Marina, The Duchess of Kent, visited the carrier to say farewell to the ship which she had launched 18 years previously. Here she meets the flight deck personnel.

(Rear-Admiral Steiner)

The *Centaur* arrives at Belfast for a farewell visit.

(Rear-Admiral Steiner)

turned out to watch the arrival of the *Britannia*. As soon as she was securely anchored, the Minister of Defence and Admiral Sir David Luce, the First Sea Lord, went on board, followed by the C-in-C Home Fleet, Admiral Sir John Frewen, together with the Provosts of Greenock and Gourock. At 10.30am the Queen and Prince Philip, accompanied by Prince Charles, Princess Anne and Prince Andrew, visited the destroyer HMS *Kent*, then the frigate *Dido*, on which 30 displays had been arranged. As well as armed landing parties there were also personnel demonstrating the asbestos suits worn when checking for radiation and nuclear contamination, and equipment and methods used in operations aimed at alleviating suffering after disasters such as earthquakes. At midday the Queen held a reception on board the *Britannia* for junior officers followed by a luncheon for the commanding officers of the assembled ships. By now the sun had broken through the mist and the leisure craft were massed thicker than ever in the lines of warships as, during the afternoon, the royal party visited the submarine depot ship HMS *Maidstone*, before going on to the Royal Navy's first and, at that time, only nuclear powered submarine, HMS *Dreadnought*. Not unnaturally, given the novelty of the submarine, the visit to *Dreadnought* received a great deal of press publicity and it tended to overshadow the royal party's next visit, which

was to the *Centaur*.

It was just before 4.30pm when the Queen and Prince Philip climbed the carrier's gangway, and although the weather was warm and moderately fair, the mist had begun to fall once again and so the tea party which was being given by the Chief Petty Officers, and which had been dubbed 'The Mad Hatter's Tea Party', was held in the hangar instead of on the flight deck. Shortly after the Queen and Prince Philip had boarded they were joined by Prince Charles and Princess Anne, and after mixing informally with the carrier's 350 CPOs the royal visitors toured the hangar display before disembarking at 5.30pm to return to the *Britannia*. That same evening the FOAC, Rear-Admiral H. R. B. Janvrin, and Captain Steiner left the ship to dine with the Queen and Prince Philip in the C-in-C's flagship, HMS *Lion*.

Wednesday 11 August dawned as damp and misty as the previous day, but this did not deter thousands more sightseers from turning out to see the *Britannia* take her leave of the Clyde as the ships' companies manned the decks to cheer ship as the Royal Yacht passed by. However, all the pomp and ceremony did not seem to impress two teenagers who were seen rowing out past the fleet, as it turned out, to start their day's fishing as they usually did at that time. As the *Britannia* left the Tail of the Bank for the

The 1965 Clyde Fleet Review, and the Royal Yacht *Britannia* arrives on a misty morning and steams through the lines of assembled warships. The cruiser *Tiger* is anchored on the *Centaur's* port bow.

(*D. Palmer*)

Her Majesty The Queen is shown around the *Centaur's* hangar display during her visit to the carrier on the afternoon of Tuesday 10 August 1965.

(*D. Palmer*)

The fleet lit up during the evening of 10 August 1965. From left to right HM Ships *Maidstone, Centaur, Tiger, Lion* and the Royal Yacht just visible on the right of the picture. *(D. Palmer)*

Pentland Firth, and as the last echoes of the 21-gun royal salute died away, the Queen sent the following signal to the C-in-C, Admiral Sir John Frewen: 'I have been greatly impressed with all that I have seen of officers and men and their ships and equipment during the two days that I have been with you in the Clyde. It gives me particular pleasure to see the RNR divisions and the Royal Fleet Auxiliaries represented here. I and my husband have much enjoyed our visit. Congratulations to you all. Splice the main brace!'. The review had been the highlight of an extremely busy commission, but now the *Centaur's* operational career was drawing to a close.

During the afternoon of Wednesday 11 August the review fleet dispersed, but it was not until the next morning that the *Centaur* weighed anchor and steamed south for Liverpool. She arrived at the mouth of the River Mersey at just after midday on Friday 13 August and at 3.45pm she was safely secured alongside the Princes Landing Stage which is overlooked by the Liver Building. That the visit was a huge success can be judged by the fact that during the two days when she was opened to the public almost 22,000 people went to view the ship. There were more than a few tears when, at 6am on Monday 16 August, the *Centaur* left Princes Pier and after a rather slow and tortuous passage downriver she anchored in Liverpool Bay, close to the Mersey Bar Light Vessel. Next day, at 12.20pm, she weighed anchor and set course for Portsmouth with 'Flying Stations' being piped for the last time at 3.15pm. Ten minutes later her aircraft complement

of one Gannet, three Sea Vixens and, finally, one Scimitar were launched for their shore stations, (three Sea Vixens of 892 Squadron were already on a detachment to RNAS Brawdy), after which Captain Steiner put his foot hard down on the accelerator and ordered full power as the 'old lady' lifted her skirts and steamed hard down the Irish Sea at almost 28 knots, with the cable deck awash and out of bounds. However, next morning thick fog in the Channel hampered her progress when speed had to be reduced drastically and it was at 6.35am on Friday 20 August that the *Centaur* secured alongside Middle Slip Jetty and 'Finished With Engines' was rung for the last time.

Soon afterwards, on a hot, sunny day, a brief but poignant paying-off service was held on the flight deck, and on Tuesday 24 August 1965 Captain Steiner, who had been promoted to Rear-Admiral, left the ship and the Executive Officer, Commander G. Y. Temple RN, took command. The public still had a chance to see the *Centaur* at first hand during Navy Days at the end of the month, and 25,584 people took the opportunity to visit the ship. During September 1965 the *Centaur's* ship's company was largely dispersed, but a few stayed on, including George Lees who still has these memories of his final weeks on board: 'After our final return to Portsmouth most of the ship's company were drafted to their next ships, but a number of us were retained on board to put the ship into mothballs. I was given the job of preserving the ship's tanks, and this was done by coating them with thick oil. At first I painted the oil on with a brush, but as each stroke

The *Centaur* alongside Middle Slip Jetty on Sunday 22 August 1965, two days after her arrival at the port.

(M. Lennon)

Soon after her arrival at the Cairnryan ship-breaker's yard a fire broke out in *Centaur's* island superstructure which took the fire brigade two days to extinguish.

(R. Holme)

covered only a few square inches, it was clear that it was going to be a long job. Someone hit on the idea of warming the oil in order to thin it down and then to apply it with paint spraying equipment. This worked very well and it was much faster than painting but, oh! what a mess we all got into. I finally left the *Centaur* at the end of 1965 and, despite the ups and downs during the commission, I will always remember her as a very happy ship.'

For the immediate future it had been decided that the *Centaur* would become an accommodation ship for the ships' companies of vessels which were undergoing major refits in the dockyard and during this time she would come under the command of the CO of whichever ship was using her for this purpose. The first such ship's company was from the *Victorious* which had started a major refit on 26 August 1965 and four weeks later, at 9am on Monday 27 September, with all the *Centaur's* stores and ammunition having been disembarked, Captain D. L. Davenport OBE RN and all the ship's company of the *Victorious* moved on board.

Work on the *Victorious* was completed in early 1966 and the *Centaur* became home to a variety of ships' companies in the months that followed. In the summer of 1967 she made the news headlines when the ship's safe containing £2,000 was stolen one night. For six months between April and September 1969 she became home to the *Hermes'* ship's company whilst their own carrier was docked down in D Lock dry dock. Seven months later, on Friday 24 April 1970, after three false starts because of weather conditions, she left Portsmouth for good in the tow of three ocean-going tugs, *Agile, Samsonia* and *Reward*, bound for Devonport where she was to accommodate the *Eagle's* ship's company for six months whilst that carrier underwent a refit. I was one of those who lived on the *Centaur* at that time and although the living spaces in use were always kept clean and tidy, I have memories of the evidence of the neglect which pervaded most of the ship. On the flight deck there were large areas of paint peeling away to reveal the rusting steel plates beneath, and inside the ship the dark, gloomy passageways were strangely silent, apart from the condensation that dripped from some of the firemain pipes. The machinery spaces were in complete darkness and by torchlight all that could be seen was the white lagging which, in places, was beginning to

A final view of the *Centaur* alongside the deep water wharf at Cairnryan before the cutting torches started their work.

(*R. Holme*)

fall away from the pipes it once protected. There were unexplained floods in some of the disused compartments and on the bridge a thick coating of dust had built up on the heavily greased brass instruments which had once been lovingly polished by each watch whilst they were on duty. She was in a very sad state and I can remember feeling somehow relieved when, in December 1970, she was put up for disposal.

For almost two years the *Centaur* was laid up at Devonport before being sold to the Queenborough Shipbreaking Company on 18 August 1972, and on Monday 4 September she left Devonport under tow of three tugs. Three days later, on Thursday 7 September, she arrived at Cairnryan, Wigtownshire, where she was secured alongside the deep water wharf, starboard side to. Already alongside the wharf was the destroyer *Saintes*, but the *Centaur* was the first of the four aircraft carriers which would end their days at Cairnryan (the others being *Eagle*, *Ark Royal* and the *Centaur's* sister ship *Bulwark*), and being

much bigger than other vessels which had been demolished there she caused the contractor some anxiety. Soon after her arrival cutting torches caused a fire in her island superstructure which took the fire brigade two days to extinguish. Despite the problems caused by her size, she was cut down very slowly and then the hull was cut back to the first bulkhead. Then, having found large tanks at both the stern and bows, the contractor flooded them to tip each end into the air in turn, thus exposing the stem and stern which were then cut away. Finally, what remained of the hull was beached and the demolition was complete.

It is fitting that the final words should go to Captain Steiner, her last commanding officer, who observed: 'Not only was *Centaur* the first carrier to be fitted with an angled flight deck, but we "invented" carrier replenishment at sea with a supply ship keeping station on both beams. It was frowned upon at the time by some "fuddy-duddies", but it has since become common practice. I commanded a superb ship's company and aircrews.'

'Finis'

Appendix One

Principal Particulars

Length Overall:	737ft
Beam Overall:	128ft
Standard Displacement:	26,118 tons
Draught:	22 ft
Armament:	26 radar controlled 40mm Bofors
Aircraft:	35 Sea Hawk/Sea Venom
Main Propulsion Machinery:	Twin screw: Two sets Parsons single-reduction geared turbines. Steam provided by four Admiralty Three Drum Boilers in two boiler rooms.
SHP:	80,000
Speed:	28 knots
Complement (with embarked squadrons):	1,330
Flight Deck:	Built with axial flight deck. Went straight from builder's yard to Portsmouth Dockyard where interim angled flight deck $5^{1}/_{2}°$ was fitted, giving a 64ft-wide landing area. Two aircraft lifts. Two catapults. Six arrester wires.
Deck Recognition Letter:	L (1953) C (1954-1965)
Pennant Number:	R06

Appendix Two

Commanding Officers HMS *Centaur*

	Date Appointed:
Captain H. P. Sears RN	13 August 1953
Captain H. C. N. Rolfe RN	17 October 1954
Captain H. R. Law OBE DSC RN	18 August 1958
Captain J. A. C. Henley DSC RN	18 August 1960
Captain P. G. Sharp DSC RN	18 June 1962
Captain O. H. M. St John Steiner RN	20 May 1963

Appendix Three

Former *Centaurs*

The First *Centaur*

A sixth-rate (24 guns) of some 504 tons, she was launched in 1746 when Britain was at war with France and the Jacobite rebellion was finally crushed by the Hanoverians led by the Duke of Cumberland at the Battle of Culloden. She was finally commissioned during the subsequent uneasy peace of 1753.

However, French interference with the British colonists of North America forced Britain to take action and thus began the Seven Years' War. The *Centaur* played her part, doing routine chores of the service but taking no part in any actions which deserve a special mention. She was finally paid off at Portsmouth in 1759 and sold to private interests.

The Second *Centaur*

A third-rate (74 guns) of 1,739 tons, she had a complement of 650. She was originally the French ship *Centaure* but was captured in the action off Lagos, Portugal, on 18 August 1759. At the time it was known that the French were collecting a force together at Toulon to send round to join the main French fleet at Brest. Although the British squadron in the Mediterranean was only small, Admiral the Hon Edward Boscawen was sent out to take over as the C-in-C. On 17 August, while the British fleet was in Gibraltar, a patrolling frigate sighted the French fleet close under the Barbary shore. Admiral Boscawen was informed immediately and a long stern chase followed. At noon on 18 August fire was opened on the last ship of the French line, which was the *Centaure*. From that moment until the evening she bore the brunt of the fight, being engaged by every British ship in turn as they came within range. At last, with her topmasts shot away, she was so badly damaged that she had no alternative but to strike her battle ensign. During the action the British fleet captured or destroyed a total of four French ships of the line for the loss of only 56 killed and 196 wounded. The *Centaure's* losses alone were 200 killed. After repairs had been carried out she was sailed to England with two other prizes, the *Temeraire* and *Modeste*, where she was purchased by the Admiralty for HM service in 1760 and registered in the Navy List by the name of *Centaur*.

In those days it was normal practice for ships which had been captured in action to be recommissioned by the victors, and this often resulted in confusion, as illustrated by the following incident. The *Centaur*, which was now established under the White Ensign, fell in with the French ships *Valliant* and *Amethyst* off Cape Finisterre, whilst homeward-bound from the West Indies. The French captains were quite obviously deceived by her appearance and they let her come close up. It was not until they saw her clearing away for action that they realized she was no longer a French ship. However, they managed to make all possible sail and escape into Corunna under cover of darkness.

By 1760 the French Navy had been soundly beaten, but British mercantile losses to small privateers were still very high and at the end of the year it was decided to increase the force stationed in the West Indies. On the death of Admiral Holmes on 21 November 1760, Captain Arthur Forrest of the *Centaur* became the senior officer of the Jamaica Station, and several single ship encounters of minor importance took place. A typical action was one where *Centaur* captured the heavily armed merchantman *St Anne*. Soon after this Spain came into the war allied with France, but, fortunately, Admiral Rodney had been able to attack Spanish trade in the West Indies before the colonial Spanish authorities knew that they were in the war.

In February 1762, whilst at Martinique, Admiral Rodney heard that a strong Spanish squadron had arrived in Havana and the British Naval Base at Jamaica was felt to be under threat. He therefore sent a frigate to warn Captain Forrest on the *Centaur*, and ordered him to join the fleet off Cape St Nicholas. However, before Rodney could take any further action, Admiral Sir George Pocock arrived from England with secret orders for the reduction of the Spanish city of Havana. It was a combined operation with both the Navy and Army involved and Havana was besieged by the expedition, which was commanded by the Earl of Albermarle. On 13 August the Spanish capitulated and stores, specie and valuables worth some £3,000,000 were taken, along with nine sail of the line. The city of Havana was occupied and the whole expedition was deemed to have won a very notable victory. The *Centaur* then helped to bring home the prizes which had been seized.

Rodney was relieved by Admiral Keppel, and when the American colonists rebelled in 1770 and he refused to fight them he was given a command at home. In 1778, by a Treaty of Alliance, France threw her weight on the side of the colonists and the French fleet of 30 sail of the line set out for America. At the time there were only six British frigates at sea and the Admiralty hastily had to assemble a fleet of 32 ships of the line and 15 frigates, under Admiral Keppel, to oppose the French expedition. On 27 July 1778 the fleets joined action off Ushant, on opposite courses. The *Centaur*, Captain P. Cosby, was the third ship in the Starboard Division under Vice-Admiral Harland, flying his flag in the *Queen*. It was this division which showed most initiative, after the first engagement, in clearing and tacking towards the enemy. Had the others showed similar good sense, Keppel could have brought his fleet to action again, but they did not, and what might have been a decisive fleet action ended in an unsatisfactory and indecisive brush.

In 1779 Spain joined France and declared war on Britain and both countries received a great deal of assistance, including stores, from 'neutral' Holland. On 31 December 1779 the *Centaur* was part of a British squadron, commanded by Captain Charles Fielding in the *Namur*, which intercepted a large Dutch convoy being escorted by two sail of the line and two frigates and which was in the charge of Rear-Admiral Van Bylandt, who declared that he would open fire if any search was attempted. Boats from the British squadron were immediately sent away and the Dutch ships opened fire. The British replied immediately and, with honour satisfied, Admiral Van Bylandt struck his flag and surrendered the convoy. No blood was shed during this exchange, but Captain Fielding returned to port with nine fully laden prize ships.

In December 1780 Admiral Rodney returned to the West Indies to find that, after some violent hurricanes, he had only nine ships available for sea. He was reinforced by Commodore Sir Samuel Hood's division of eight ships, which included the *Centaur*, and with Holland now being firmly allied to the French and Spanish, he received orders to seize Dutch possessions in the area. He sailed at once for St Eustatious, 50 miles north of the British colony of St Kitts, and on his arrival the Dutch island immediately capitulated, after which Rodney stayed on for three months to 'administer' the £3,000,000 prize booty.

Meanwhile, the French at Brest were preparing a very large convoy, to be protected by 21 sail of the line commanded by Admiral de Grasse, and Hood was ordered to intercept them. On 29 April 1781 de Grasse sailed round Salt Point south of Martinique, at which stage Hood was badly placed, being too far to leeward. Unable to overtake the French ships, Hood shortened sail, hoping to bring the enemy down upon him and he was not disappointed for de Grasse released his convoy and turned onto a southerly tack. Four of the British ships, including the *Centaur*, were attacked by eight French vessels and they suffered considerable damage to their hulls and spars. Captain Nott of the *Centaur* was killed, but in the whole action the British ships lost only 39 killed and 162 wounded, whilst the French losses were 119 killed and 150 wounded.

On 2 July 1781 Rear-Admiral Thomas Graves assumed command of the North American Station and Hood was ordered there as well when intelligence was received that French ships at Newport were to be reinforced by de Grasse's West Indian fleet. Altogether Graves had 19 ships of the line, including the *Centaur*, commanded by Captain John N. Inglefield. They sailed on 31 August for Chesapeake where, it was thought, the French fleet and the combined armies of Washington and Rochambeau were assembling. However, de Grasse, with 24 ships of the line, arrived first and it was not until 5 September that a French picket off Cape Henry sighted the British fleet. The ensuing action was claimed as a victory by each of the adverseries and the British lost 90 killed and 246 wounded, while the French lost 200 killed and an unknown number of wounded.

The following year, on 16 January, de Grasse laid siege to St Kitts and Hood went to the rescue with 22 sail of the line, including the *Centaur*. The subsequent victory won by Hood is considered by many historians to be equal to anything that Nelson later achieved. The French were ousted from their anchorage and replaced by Hood's ships and despite being counter-attacked again and again, he finally beat them into submission. However, the British garrison ashore was outnumbered by three to one and they were unable to hold out against the French. Admiral de Grasse had called up reinforcements and, having 32 ships of the line, he waited for Hood to sail. However, Hood was able to trick him whilst storing at the nearby island of Nevis, when his ships stole silently away.

The enemy's next step was to be the conquest of Jamaica, but this involved the escort of a convoy of supply ships and Rodney was very much aware of all the preparation and so kept up constant patrols in the area. On 8 April 1782 this vigilance was rewarded when his lookout patrol sighted a convoy of 150 merchantmen escorted by 35 sail of the line off Dominica. The ensuing action took place between Dominica and Guadeloupe near a group of islands called The Saints, which gave their name to the battle. By 6am on 9 April the French fleet and convoy were visible from the *Centaur* which was part of the van of Rodney's fleet of 36 ships of the line. The French were extended from abreast the west side of the centre of Dominica, northwards towards Guadeloupe. The wind was from the east, but only those ships which had already cleared Dominica's high northern shore could feel the fresh trade winds and had freedom of manoeuvre. Hood's division were the first of the British ships to clear and de Grasse lost a wonderful opportunity to annihilate it before the rest of the British fleet could clear Dominica, which would have left him with the advantage. However, in the event, because de Grasse wanted to deter pursuit of his convoy, he declined to stay and fight, and only sent half of his fleet against Hood's ships.

The British squadron, including *Centaur*, sustained some damage, but not enough to cripple their sailing power and Rodney put them to the rear and doggedly held on in pursuit of the French. Hood's squadron had, in fact, inflicted such damage on the French ships, that in the next two days four of them fell astern and became detached. In an attempt to rescue two of them, the *Zele* and the *Magnanime*, de Grasse became inescapably committed to action and the first shots were fired at 8am on 12 April. Once again superior British tactics brought about the French defeat, and the French flagship *Ville de Paris*, the biggest man-of-war then afloat (110 guns), struck, as did the *Glorieux, Hector, Cesar* and *Ardent*.

At the end of July 1782, Rear-Admiral Graves in *Ramilles*, with *Centaur, Canada*, and *Pallas*, all left Jamaica with the prizes and 180 merchantmen. Unfortunately, the men-of-war were in poor condition, particularly the *Centaur*. She had been in the service of the Royal Navy for 22 years and when, on 16 September, the fleet ran into a severe east-south-easterly storm off the Banks of Newfoundland there was scarcely a man-of-war that was not dismasted. The *Ramilles* lost her main mizzen and was finally abandoned and set on fire by her crew, while the *Centaur* lost all her masts and her rudder. When she heeled to the squall, the water burst between the decks and she became a waterlogged hulk, settling slowly. It was a tragic end for a splendid old ship which had served the country so well in the service of the Royal Navy. Her captain, J. N. Inglefield, left in the pinnace with 11 others and after enduring incredible privation reached the Azores 16 days later.

The Third *Centaur*

Built at Woolwich, the next *Centaur* was another third-rate (74 guns) of 1,842 tons with a complement of 640, and she was launched on 14 March 1797 and commissioned later that year.

The background to her career is the Napoleonic Wars when, after the Battle of the Nile in 1798, Napoleon concentrated on his land campaign. Spain's attitude at this time was increasingly lukewarm and it deteriorated even more after St Vincent's blockade of Cadiz. The blockade was uneventful and in the autumn of 1798 St Vincent detached a squadron under Commodore J. T. Duckworth, flying his broad pendant in HMS *Leviathan*, against the island of Minorca. The *Centaur*, Captain Thomas Markham, was one of the ships of this squadron and she had troops on board under the command of General the Hon Charles Stuart. On 9 November Fort Carlos surrendered and four days later Duckworth defeated a small Spanish squadron which had appeared and, in the process, recaptured the former British sloop *Petrel*. On 15 November the island garrison of 3,500 men surrendered and General Stuart was made a KB. However, Commodore Duckworth received no reward whatsoever, nor did Captain Markham of the *Centaur*.

On 16 March 1799, while on patrol with the *Cormorant*, in the vicinity of Cape Oropesa, the *Centaur* came up with the 42-gun Spanish ship *Guadelupe*, which promptly fled. However, the British ship gave chase and finally drove her ashore and destroyed her.

For some time the French Minister of Marine, Admiral Bruix, had been preparing a fleet at Brest with the object of reinforcing the Toulon naval base and driving the British out of the Mediterranean, and on 25 April 1799 he sailed with 25 ships of the line, reinforced with 17 Spanish vessels. Despite a lengthy search, Admiral Lord Keith was never able to catch up with the enemy fleet, but during the operations to find them the *Centaur* and *Montague* captured a number of small craft from which they learned the whereabouts of the French. However, before Lord Keith could recommence the search, he received orders to return to Rosas Bay and whilst on the passage, about 60 miles south of Cape Sicie, his advance squadron, including *Centaur*, *Bellona*, *Captain*, *Emerald* and *Santa Teresa*, captured a French squadron which included the flagship of Rear-Admiral Perree.

Peace was signed at Amiens in March 1802, but war was renewed in 1803 and, as often happened in those days, an extension of Britain's overseas possessions followed.

On 21 June 1803, Commodore Sir Samuel Hood, flying his broad pendant in the *Centaur* (Captain Littlehales), and with a number of other vessels carrying troops under Lt-General Grinfield, anchored in Choc Bay, St Lucia. The troops were landed and soon afterwards they took the town of Castries. Next day the fortress of Morne Fortunee was stormed and captured and soon after this the island capitulated. Then the *Centaur*, with some small craft and troops, sailed on 25 June for Tobago where she arrived six days later. The troops were then landed and soon afterwards the French garrison surrendered. Subsequently the Dutch colonies of Demerara, Essequibo and Berberice were captured. To the south-west of Martinique lies the islet of Diamond Rock which is roughly the shape of a haystack, rising sharply and precipitously from the sea. It is about one mile in circumference and its highest point is some 600 feet above sea level. Only from the west is access possible from the sea, but the rock offered excellent opportunities for commerce raiders which could harass the French ships which ran in and out of Port Royal, and in January 1804 it was seized by a party of men from the *Centaur*. Guns and ammunition were landed and one of the *Centaur's* officers, Lieutenant James W. Maurice RN, took command of the base which was commissioned as the 'sloop' HMS *Diamond Rock*, and which was manned by 120 of her ship's company.

Early in February 1804 Commodore Hood was determined to destroy the French brig *Curieux* which was lying in the harbour of Port Royal and which was almost ready for sea. On 3 February 60 seamen and 12 marines from the *Centaur*, commanded by Lieutenant R. Reynolds RN, rowed in four boats for 20 miles in order to make an attack. However, the French had anticipated such a move and they had loaded all their guns with grapeshot and posted additional sentries. As it was a bright moonlit night the boats were seen long before they could get close and the *Curieux* fired her guns at them, but with little effect, perhaps because the Royal Marines kept up a steady fire as they were rowed into the harbour. Fortunately, the first boat found a rope ladder which had been carelessly left hanging under the stern of the French ship. The British marines and the sailors, (this was after the latter had rowed for some 20 miles), clambered aboard and began hand-to-hand fighting. Eventually the French crew were overpowered and the brig was made ready for sea by its new British company, who came under fire from French shore batteries as they left harbour. The British had lost three officers and six seamen, but the French casualties were so high that Hood sent them back to Port Royal in the *Curieux* under a flag of truce. On her return to the British fleet, Lieutenant Reynolds was given command of the *Curieux*, but he died soon afterwards of wounds which he had received in the fight to capture the ship. He was posthumously awarded a Bar to his General Service Medal for this exploit.

Two months later, on 25 April 1804, Commodore Hood in *Centaur*, commanding a small British squadron, arrived off the Dutch island of Surinam and landed 700 men to capture the Dutch base. It was not long before Fort Nieuw Amsterdam surrendered, followed then by the whole colony and some 2,000 prisoners and 282 guns were taken.

The *Centaur* finally left the West Indies and on 15 July 1806 boats from the squadron of which she formed part, attempted to cut out two corvettes and a convoy sheltering in the Gironde River. They succeeded in carrying off one of the corvettes, the *Cesar*, but it was at considerable cost to themselves, having suffered nine killed, 39 wounded and 20 taken prisoner. For this action a Bar to the Naval General Service Medal was awarded.

On 24 September five French frigates and two corvettes were bound for the West Indies with stores and troops on board. However, Hood's squadron, which included the *Centaur*, intercepted the French ships and after a fierce fight they captured the enemy vessels. The British force suffered casualties of nine killed and 29 wounded, among the latter being Commodore Hood, who lost an arm.

After the Battle of Trafalgar in October 1805, Napoleon had abandoned his proposed invasion of England and had forced Russia and Prussia into the war as his allies. The *Centaur's* next action was a long way away from the warm waters of the West Indies. In July 1807 Britain decided on the rather bold move of 'inviting' Denmark to hand over her fleet, with an undertaking that it would be restored on the conclusion of hostilities. In order to give the Danes some incentive Admiral James Gambier sailed with some 25 ships of the line into the Baltic, and included in the fleet was the *Centaur*, commanded by Captain W. H. Webley RN and once again flying the broad pendant of Commodore Hood. As expected the Danes refused to surrender their fleet, and the British ships commenced the bombardment of Copenhagen which resulted in the near demolition of the city. However, Admiral Gambier secured most of the Danish fleet of 16 ships of the line and over 50 smaller vessels.

That same year Napoleon demanded of Portugal that she close her ports to British commerce and as a result Sir Sydney Smith's squadron 'rescued' the Portuguese royal family and took them to Brazil, while a squadron commanded by Commodore Hood in the *Centaur*, with troops under Major-General W. Beresford, sailed to Madeira, effected an unopposed landing and took over the island.

In 1808, with Russia and Denmark now ranged with France, it seemed prudent to send a strong expedition to support Britain's only Baltic ally, Sweden, and at the end of May that year a force of 17 ships under Vice-Admiral Sir James Saumarez in *Victory*, with Hood, who was now a Rear-Admiral, in *Centaur*, sailed for the Baltic. In early August a Russian fleet of over 70 ships left their base at Kronstadt and anchored off Oresund. The *Centaur* was also at the port together with HMS *Implacable* (74 guns) and nine Swedish sail of the line. However, on board both the British and Swedish ships at least one-third of the crews were sick with scurvy. Nevertheless, Hood weighed anchor and it was not long before the British ships caught up with the 74-gun Russian ship *Sevolod*, and within half an hour the British ships had forced her to surrender. However, Hood, fearing that they might be overwhelmed by the large Russian fleet, recalled the *Centaur* before she could take possession of her prize. This was followed by a period of indecision during which the Russian Admiral took the opportunity to get the *Sevolod* in tow, but the *Centaur* and *Implacable* again closed and soon the tow was abandoned. The Russians declined a general engagement and made off, leaving the *Sevolod* to run aground on a shoal outside the harbour and soon afterwards she was refloated and left to ride at anchor there. The Russian Admiral then sent away numerous boats to try to tow the *Sevolod* into harbour. While this operation was in progress the *Centaur*, thanks to the excellent seamanship of her officers and men, managed to run alongside and board the Russian ship where they were met by a withering fire from the Russian ship's guns. Not deterred by this, Captain Webley, Lieutenant Lawless and Mister Edward Strode (Master) lashed what was left of the *Sevolod's* bowsprit to the *Centaur's* mizzen rigging, thereby hoping to tow off the Russian ship. Unfortunately, the *Sevolod's* anchors held her fast and it required the threat of further intervention from the *Implacable* to force the surrender of the Russian ship which, for the second time, hauled down her colours. During the action the *Centaur* had three killed and 27 wounded, and the *Sevolod* suffered 180 killed, wounded and missing. By the time the action ended both the *Sevolod* and the *Centaur* were grounded, but the *Implacable* pulled her consort into deeper water while the *Sevolod* was set on fire and destroyed. For this action a Bar to the Naval General Service Medal was awarded.

After the partial destruction of the French fleet in Aix Roads in 1810 there were few major actions, but a number of small skirmishes occurred and on 6 April 1814, with the Allies in Paris, the *Centaur*, commanded by Captain John White, entered the Gironde River with the intention of attacking ships which were lying under the protection of the shore batteries. However, French morale was very low and at the sight of the *Centaur* they set fire to their own flotilla.

The *Centaur* remained in commission for four years after the peace of 1815, before being demolished at Devonport.

The Fourth *Centaur*

For over a generation after the final defeat of Napoleon there were no major wars which involved Britain, although the Royal Navy was occupied in many small campaigns against pirates in the South China Seas and against the slave traders of the West African coast.

Built at Portsmouth and launched on 6 October 1845, the fourth *Centaur* was one of the first paddle wheel steam frigates, with machinery that gave her 540 HP, and armed with six guns.

In 1849 she was engaged in many successful expeditions against pirates in the River Seba, with Captain C. Buckle RN in command, and flying the broad pendant of Commodore Arthur Fanshawe. Between 1849 and 1854 she was successively flagship on the West Coast of Africa Station and on the East Coast of South America.

On 27 March 1854 Britain and France declared war on Russia and in the second Baltic campaign of 1855, *Centaur*, commanded by Captain William J. Clifford RN, formed part of the fleet under Rear-Admiral the Hon R. S. Dundas, the first force to be made up wholly of steam-powered vessels. Records mention the *Centaur*, with the *Imperieuse* and *Bulldog*, having a long-range engagement with batteries and gunboats in the vicinity of Tolboukin Lighthouse, off Kronstadt, on 16 August 1855.

Hostilities ended with the Treaty of Paris in 1856 and in April that year, in celebration, Queen Victoria, on board the Royal Yacht *Victoria and Albert*, reviewed the fleet at Spithead. The *Centaur* was one of the 18 paddle craft which took part in the review.

At this time there was considerable unrest in China and in the Second China War of 1860, rocket boats from the *Centaur* co-operated in the taking of the Taku Forts in the Peiho River, which was one of the contributory actions which led to the final march on Peking.

In 1861 there followed the Taiping Rebellion and Britain, with all her interests in China, had some clashes with the Taiping forces. In May 1862 the Taiping rebels were making a determined effort to capture Soonking, but they were repulsed by a landing party from the *Centaur* which was assisting government forces. However, on 2 June the Taiping rebels won a victory outside the town and they captured a gig from the *Centaur*, together with a number of Chinese gunboats, but a sortie from the *Centaur* recaptured the gig and most of the gunboats.

The fourth *Centaur* was broken up at Devonport in 1865.

Appendix Four

HMS *Centaur* 1915-1934

The fifth *Centaur* was built by Vickers as the name ship of a class of two light cruisers (the second being HMS *Concord*), and her hull was laid down on 24 January 1915. They were additional units of the 1914-15 building programme and they were often referred to as the 'Turkish' ships, because the builder was authorized to use the main propulsion machinery which had been intended for two Turkish scout cruisers. The *Centaur* was a light cruiser of 3,750 tons and she was completed and first commissioned in August 1916. She and her sister were equipped with five 6-inch guns and when the *Centaur* joined the Harwich Force she was nicknamed 'Tyrwhitt's Dreadnought'.

The *Centaur's* first action which is worthy of mention came in the early part of 1917. During the forenoon of 22 January, the Admiralty received intelligence that the German 6th Destroyer Flotilla would be leaving for Zeebrugge sometime that afternoon and the duty of intercepting the enemy ships fell on the Harwich Force which had been reinforced by units from the Grand Fleet. Commodore Tyrwhitt, flying his broad pendant in *Centaur*, was ordered to intercept with destroyers and to use his cruisers in a support role. Despite a most careful disposition of his force in patrol lines, only the *Centaur's* division was engaged in action with the enemy, Contact was made in the early hours of 23 January and the *Centaur* immediately opened fire. The leader of the German Flotilla, V69, was struck and her helm jammed. As she turned in a circle she was rammed by G41, which was so badly damaged that she had to reduce her speed to eight knots. The remainder of the German Flotilla escaped under cover of a thick smokescreen.

In the same year, after the successful bombardment of Zeebrugge, Admiral Bacon decided to repeat the operation with a similar bombardment of Ostend Dockyard. At 10pm on 4 June, a bombardment squadron of two monitors, two flotilla leaders and six destroyers made for the Outer Ratel Bank. An hour earlier Commodore Tyrwhitt, in the *Centaur*, with three other light cruisers and nine destroyers, left Harwich to cover the action from the Thornton Bank. He reached his patrol station at 2.15am and 15 minutes later sighted two destroyers ahead. These opened fire immediately and at once came under the crushing concentration of fire from the *Centaur* and the other British ships. With one enemy destroyer sunk and the other hopelessly damaged, the bombardment was a complete success.

The *Centaur* remained with the Harwich Force, engaged primarily on patrol work, until the Armistice. In the post-war years the *Centaur* and her sister ship were partially disarmed, with the *Centaur* having her second 6-inch gun replaced by a deckhouse. From March 1919 until October 1923 she formed part of the Mediterranean Fleet's Light Cruiser Squadron, recommissioning at Malta in June 1920 and at Gibraltar in March 1922. In the autumn of 1923 she was paid off into reserve at Devonport.

During 1924-25 she was refitted, and was recommissioned at Portsmouth on 8 April 1925, as Commodore (D) Atlantic Fleet. She was recommissioned in February 1928 and, finally, in September 1930. She paid off into reserve at Portsmouth in March 1932 and in 1933 she was placed on the sales list. In February 1934 she was finally sold for breaking up.

The fifth *Centaur* was built during the Great War of 1914-18 and she saw action against the German High Seas Fleet. This photograph shows her in the mid-1920s.

118

(Maritime Photo Library)

HMS *Centaur*
Celeriter Ferox
(*Swiftly Fierce*)

Battle Honours:

Havana	1762	Curieux	1804
The Saints	1782	Baltic	1855
St Kitts	1782	Sevolod	1808
Minorca	1798	China	1860

Belgian Coast 1916-17

Acknowledgements:

My thanks to Rear-Admiral O. H. J. St John Steiner CB, the *Centaur's* last operational commanding officer, for his help and for kindly writing the foreword to this book. My thanks also to Mrs Dilys Sharp JP, the widow of the late Rear-Admiral Philip Sharp, and to two more of *Centaur's* commanding officers as follows, Rear-Admiral H. C. N. Rolfe CB and Admiral Sir Horace Law GCB.

I must also thank the following for their contributions to the book, and in many cases for the loan of photographs:-
Jim Allaway, Editor, *Navy News*: Peter Ames, Bodmin, Cornwall: Kenneth Anderson, Ulster Folk Museum, Holywood, Belfast: A. N. Bailey, Witham Friary, Somerset: Roger Beacham, Cheltenham Reference Library: Ronald Bennett, Cromer, Norfolk: Terry Brown, Bexleyheath, Kent: Michael Cassar, Valletta, Malta: Michael Coles, Swindon, Wiltshire: Lt-Cdr Arthur J. D. Coxon RN (Retd), Dinas Powys, Vale of Glamorgan: Geoffrey Dewsbury, Swansea: Horace C. Edwards, Sheerness, Kent: Carol Farr, Librarian, *The News*, Portsmouth: Peter Harris, Wath-upon-Dearne, South Yorkshire: Jim Harper, Coventry, Warwickshire: Richard Holme, Tunbridge Wells, Kent: David Hooper, Rochester, Kent: R. Horsman, Tiverton, Devon: Brian Lawrence, Bexley, Kent: George Lees, Comrie, Perthshire: Michael Lennon, Waterlooville, Hampshire: Steven Mathis, Northfield, Birmingham: Geoffrey Morter, Gorlestone-on-Sea, Norfolk: Brian Mulcock BEM, Croydon, Surrey: Eric Payne, Cinderford, Gloucestershire: M. K. Pagan, Sandown, Isle of Wight: David F. Palmer, Peacehaven, Sussex: N. E. D. Parkinson, HMS *Bulwark* Association, Portsmouth: A. J. Perrett, Gosport, Hampshire: David Richardson, Research Officer, Fleet Air Arm Museum, RNAS Yeovilton, Somerset: D. W. Sexby, Northleach, Gloucestershire: F. R. Sherlock, Southampton, Hampshire: Kenneth Smith, Eastbourne, Sussex: Denis J. Sparrow, Stroud, Gloucestershire: Ian Spashett, FotoFlite, New Romney, Kent: R. J. Stapleton, Ilchester, Somerset: Donald Webber, Gosport, Hampshire: Adrian Vicary, Cromer, Norfolk: Paul Yockney, Helston, Cornwall.

Special Thanks To:
Mr Brian Conroy, Greatham, Hampshire for his watercolour painting used on the dust jacket.
Mr Ian Spashett, FotoFlite, Littlestone Road, New Romney, Kent TN28 8LW, for providing the photographs of the SS *Johan Van Oldenbarnevelt* and the SS *Lakonia*. Readers who are interested in purchasing such photographs can contact Ian at FotoFlite who have a huge selection of photographs in their collection showing post-war warships and merchant vessels.
Mr John S. Morris, Dalgety Bay, Fife, who kindly drew the ink sketch used on the endpapers.
Mr David Richardson, formerly Research Officer at the Fleet Air Arm Museum, RNAS Yeovilton, Somerset. A visit to the museum is a 'must' for anyone who is interested in the history of the Fleet Air Arm.
Mr Adrian Vicary, Maritime Photo Library, 8 Jetty Street, Cromer, Norfolk. Adrian has a large collection of photographs showing Royal Navy warships from the 19th century to the present day. Readers who are interested in purchasing such photographs should contact him for copies of his extensive lists.
My wife Freda and my two daughters Caroline and Louise for their invaluable help.